Managing

Conflict Dynamics:

A PRACTICAL APPROACH

Sal Capobianco, Ph.D.
Professor of Psychology
Eckerd College

Mark H. Davis, Ph.D.
Professor of Psychology
Eckerd College

Linda A. Kraus, Ph.D.
Mediator

Published by: Eckerd College Leadership Development Institute

To reach the Leadership Development Institute at Eckerd College:

4200 54th Avenue South
St. Petersburg, FL 33711
phone: 888-359-9906 • fax: 727-864-7575
ldi@eckerd.edu • www.eckerd.edu/ldi
www.conflictdynamics.org

ISBN# 0-9764173-0-8

LEADERSHIP
DEVELOPMENT
INSTITUTE
at
ECKERD COLLEGE

Table of Contents

Introduction

Using *Managing Conflict Dynamics*

Approach each new problem not with a view of finding what you hope will be there, but to get the truth, the realities that must be grappled with.

Bernard M. Baruch

Conflict in life is inevitable. Whether in the workplace, home or social gatherings, conflict results from the inescapable fact that people have different (and sometimes opposing) goals, needs, desires, responsibilities, perceptions, and ideas. Despite our best efforts to prevent it, we will undoubtedly find ourselves in disagreements with other people. We cannot prevent conflict entirely, nor would we want to, since some kinds of conflict can be productive.

The goal then is to try to manage conflict in such a way that its useful functions can develop, while more "toxic" forms of conflict are minimized or avoided entirely. What largely separates conflict from destructive conflict is how the involved individuals respond when the conflict occurs. **Thus, while conflict itself is inevitable, ineffective and harmful responses to conflict can be avoided, and effective and beneficial responses to conflict can be learned.** This proposition is at the heart of *Managing Conflict Dynamics: A Practical Approach.*

The Dynamics of Conflict

For our purposes, *conflict* refers to any situation in which people have incompatible interests, goals, principles, or feelings. This is, of course, a broad definition and encompasses many different situations. A conflict could arise, for instance, over a long-standing set of issues, a difference of opinion about strategy or tactics in the accomplishment of some business goal, incompatible beliefs, competition for resources, and so on. Conflicts can also result when one person acts in a way that another individual sees as insensitive, thoughtless, or rude. A conflict, in short, can result from anything that places you and another person in opposition to one another.

Particularly important to our conceptualization is the idea that conflict is **dynamic**. That is, conflict is an active process with (often) a beginning, middle, and end, a process with energy and force, capable of movement and change. Conflict may proceed slowly at times, then suddenly and quickly move in a different direction. Because it revolves around social interaction, how and where this process leads is dependent upon the participants. One's responses to a provocation can determine whether a conflict moves in a beneficial or harmful direction.

Although conflict is inevitable, this is not necessarily bad as some kinds of conflict can be beneficial. Conflict that focuses on ideas, rather than on the personalities and shortcomings of the people involved, can result in creativity, and improved group relations. Conflict that focuses on people, on the other hand, can escalate rapidly and unpleasantly, and have quite detrimental and far-reaching effects. **Table 1** outlines both the beneficial and costly consequences of conflict.

Table 1: Potential Consequences of Conflict

Potential Benefits of Conflict	Potential Costs of Conflict
• Stimulates creativity and problem-solving. • Fosters teamwork and improves social relationships. • Encourages listening and perspective taking. • Promotes reflective thinking and open communication. • Yields information about people and situations. • Signals that changes are necessary in relationships or the organization. • Provides the means for expressing emotions which can ultimately clear the air and reduce tension.	• Produces poor quality decisions. • Poisons relationships and workplace with misunderstanding and distrust. • Disrupts self, others and workplace. • Causes anger, fear, defensiveness, negativity, hurt and embarrassment. • Detrimental to building lasting relationships. • Inhibits open communication. • Lessens joint and individual outcomes. • Instigates aggression and retaliation. • Harms reputations. • Derails careers.

Responding to Conflict

Conflict is generally most beneficial when the emphasis is on issues and problem-solving, and most detrimental when focused on personalities and competition. If fair rules of conflict are followed in combination with flexibility, a concern for others and an emphasis on finding solutions, conflict can be beneficial. The goal of conflict management is to minimize the occurrence and escalation of harmful conflict while allowing the useful forms of conflict to unfold.

How can this goal be achieved? Some behavioral responses to conflict, whether occurring at the earliest stages or after the conflict develops, can be thought of as constructive. These *constructive responses* have the effect of not escalating the conflict further. They tend to reduce the tension and keep the conflict focused on ideas rather than personalities. *Destructive responses*, on the other hand, tend to make things worse; they do little to reduce the conflict and allow it to focus on personalities. If conflict can be thought of as a fire, then constructive responses help put the fire out, while destructive responses fan the flames. Obviously, it is better to respond to conflict with constructive rather than destructive responses.

It is also useful to view responses to conflict not simply as constructive or destructive, but as differing in terms of how active or passive they are. *Active responses* are those in which the individual takes some overt action in response to the conflict or provocation. Such responses can be either constructive or destructive; what makes them active is that they require some overt effort on the part of the individual. *Passive responses*, in contrast, do not require much in the way of effort from the person. In fact, they typically involve the person deciding to refrain from some kind of action. Again, passive responses can be either constructive or destructive; that is, they can make things better or they can make things worse.

Given that responses are constructive or destructive as well as active or passive, we can view responses to conflict as falling into one of four categories. **Table 2** describes these four categories and lists the types of specific actions our research indicates are common in workplace conflicts.

Table 2: Responding to Conflict

Types of Responses	Definition	Specific Actions
Active-Constructive	Through some effort on the individual's part, the conflict and tension have been reduced.	Perspective Taking Creating Solutions Expressing Emotions Reaching Out
Passive-Constructive	Although there has not been overt action by the individual, the conflict has been dampened or de-escalated.	Reflective Thinking Delay Responding Adapting
Active-Destructive	Due to some action on the individual's part, the conflict has escalated.	Winning at all Costs Displaying Anger Demeaning Others Retaliating
Passive-Destructive	Due to lack of effort or action, the individual causes conflict either to continue or to be resolved unsatisfactorily.	Avoiding Yielding Hiding Emotions Self-Criticizing

Contending with Provocation

Another important feature of our approach is the concept of **Hot Buttons** — those situations and individuals that you find especially annoying, frustrating or upsetting. When pushed, Hot Buttons can provoke you into starting or escalating a conflict. The "hottest" Hot Buttons (that is, those that are most upsetting) will be the ones most likely to evoke a quick and automatic set of destructive responses, while the "cooler" Buttons are more likely to evoke a mixture of responses that include some constructive behaviors. By learning about the situations in which you are most likely to feel upset, you can better avoid conflicts in the future. By understanding and examining the links between provocation and response, you can better control your behavior.

Conflict Dynamics Profile®

Drawing upon theoretical work, academic research and popular press writings, we have identified particular behaviors in which individuals typically engage during a conflict. Some of these behaviors exacerbate situations and make escalation into harmful conflict more likely, while others can interrupt that cycle and reduce conflict and its likelihood of escalation. Using these behaviors and based on our research findings, we developed the **Conflict Dynamics Profile®** (or **CDP**), a scale designed to help you better understand the way you typically respond to conflict in the workplace and to help you improve those areas that are most problematic.

The way in which the **CDP** does this is by measuring your behavior from several different vantage points. First, the **CDP** asks you to describe how you think you respond before, during, and after conflict. Second, the **CDP** asks other people — specifically, your boss, peers, and direct reports — how they see you responding before, during, and after conflict. The purpose of asking the same questions of many different people is to highlight any differences that may exist between the way you see your behavior and the way your friends and colleagues see it. Some of the most powerful information you will ever receive comes from learning about such differences. Because this design describes the full panorama of your behavior, it is referred to as a 360-degree scale.

In addition, the **Conflict Dynamics Profile®** provides information on two other factors related to conflict in the workplace. *Organizational Perspective On Conflict* establishes the kinds of behaviors within your particular organization that have the most negative effect on an individual's career. *Hot*

Buttons asks about some of the kinds of people and situations that are likely to upset you and subsequently may cause conflict to occur. In short, the **CDP** provides a complete "conflict profile" of you by providing feedback on:
- What provokes you.
- How you perceive the way you typically respond to conflict.
- How others view you as responding to conflict.
- Which responses to conflict have the potential to harm your position in your organization.

Once your conflict profile has been established, you will be able to clearly see those areas in which improvement is needed. Better conflict management is the goal of this book, and the focus is particularly on those areas in which you have the most control — contending with provocation and appropriately responding to conflict.

Using the Resources

The **Resources** section lists conflict-related web sites, readings and seminars. Should you desire additional information or advice or wish to further improve your conflict resolution skills, *Resources* would give you a place to begin exploring options. We do not endorse any of these seminars, readings, or web sites; we have simply provided them for your convenience.

We also encourage you to explore our web site **www.conflictdynamics.org.** Here you will find updated resources, links to useful web sites, and additional information regarding conflict, conflict management, and the **Conflict Dynamics Profile®**.

■

And One More Thing ...

We strongly recommend that you read all of ***Managing Conflict Dynamics: A Practical Approach***, not merely those pages to which you've been directed based on your ***CDP*** scores. Conflict and conflict resolution are complex issues comprised of many smaller, closely-linked matters. Due to the intertwining of these topics, and because we have tried not to be repetitive, you will get the most out of this guide by studying it in its entirety. All the information, advice and activities are described in a cookbook-like format that is easy to understand and follow. **Table 3** outlines the many unique and handy features of this guide.

Table 3: Features of This Guide

Developing Your Action Plan	Worksheets to aid you in identifying your clearest opportunities for development and tips on how develop realistic goals and a workable plan.
Before, During, And After Conflict	Hundreds of thoughts, words, behaviors, how-to's and don't-do's related to provocation and conflict at all stages. Emphasis is on learning appropriate ways to resolve conflict while building strong interpersonal relationships.
Reflection Questions	Appraisal and assessment of past conflicts, what provoked them, how you felt, how you behaved, why, what lies ahead, and how you want to respond.
Assess Yourself	Assessment after the conflict of how you did, what worked, what didn't, how others might view you and your actions, and if conflict remains, why?
Seek Feedback	Solicitation of feedback, advice and alternative points-of-view from colleagues and coaches.
Follow Up	How to respond now to the person with whom you were in conflict, particularly if the conflict remains unresolved.
Be a Role Model	How to avoid pushing other people's Hot Buttons.
Mottos	Words of encouragement and advice to inspire you and strengthen your resolve in times of crises and conflicts.
Dynamic Facts	Interesting information about Hot Buttons derived from our research.
Resources	Web sites, readings and seminars that can provide additional information and training related to the topics.

USING *MANAGING CONFLICT DYNAMICS: A PRACTICAL APPROACH*

Chapter II

Developing Your Conflict Dynamics Plan

First say to yourself what you would be; and then do what you have to do.

Epictetus

An action plan defines what you want to be and how you will get there. With it, you organize and outline your goals and strategies, anticipate potential obstacles, and set target dates. Just as an organization develops goals and plans that guide its direction and decision-making, your Action Plan will guide you. An Action Plan is, in essence, a personalized version of an organization's strategic vision. The main difference is that an Action Plan is much more specific and limited in scope.

Developing your Conflict Dynamics Action Plan will take thought and effort on your part. Following through will require even more from you: commitment, motivation, perseverance and patience. You are, after all, striving to alter behaviors, emotions and perceptions that you've held for many years, perhaps even since childhood. Changing how you view and manage conflict, and learning to confront it constructively are going to take time. This will be a process, not an event — a journey, not a step. The Developmental Worksheets will help you choose your destination, while your Action Plan will be your road map. Plan realistically, anticipate roadblocks, and be patient with detours, but most of all, get going!

CDP Developmental Worksheets

Using the information you received throughout your **CDP Feedback Report**, fill out the **CDP Developmental Worksheet: Responses to Conflict** on Page 11.

(An additional copy of this worksheet is also included in your **CDP Feedback Report**.)

- "Area of Strength" means others view you as being especially skilled at responding to conflict in this manner. Indicate in the appropriate columns what your boss, peers, and direct reports view as your strengths.

- "Opportunity for Development" means others view you as needing to improve this particular response to conflicts. Indicate in the appropriate columns the responses that, according to your boss, peers, and direct reports, are in need of development.

- Under "Highest Priority to Develop" rank the three methods of responding to conflict that your boss, peers, and direct reports view as being most in need of development. Prioritize based on their feedback in the *Responses to Conflict Profiles* (pages 7-12 of the **Feedback Report**) and the *Organizational Perspective on Conflict* (page 17 of the **Feedback Report**).

Using your *Hot Buttons Profile*, fill in the **CDP Developmental Worksheet: Hot Buttons** on Page 12. (An additional copy of this worksheet is also included in your **CDP Feedback Report**.)

- In the first column, record your Hot Button scores.

- In the second column, rank-order the three Hot Buttons that are most in need of cooling, taking into consideration:

- Your level of frustration and irritation (that is, your score).

- How frequently this Hot Button provokes you into conflict.
- The degree to which provocation of this Hot Button interferes with your job performance.

- The degree to which provocation of this Hot Button interferes with your physical and emotional well-being.

- The Hot Button ranked Number 1 should be the Hot Button that you most want (or need) to cool.

Conflict Dynamics Action Plan: Dynamic Goal

Based on what you learned about yourself from the **CDP Feedback Report** and the **CDP Developmental Worksheets**, establish your goals.
- What changes are of greatest priority?

- What actions will most address others' concerns?

- What changes if not made will be detrimental to your career in your organization

_____

_____

_____

_____

_____

_____

_____

_____

Be realistic about what you can accomplish.
- Plan a limited focus — no more than three goals at a time.

- Don't set your goals so high that you will fail.

- Ask yourself: "Is this doable? Can I realistically achieve these goals?"

Conflict Dynamics Action Plan: Constructive Action to Take

Using **Managing Conflict Dynamics: A Practical Approach** for your targeted goals, map out the action to be taken on a **Conflict Dynamics Action Plan** form. Three blank forms and one sample are provided.

- Take small, limited steps — the smaller, the better.

- Plan specific actions — the more specific, the better.

- Keep your Action Plan where you'll be reminded of it daily.

- Vow to take some goal-oriented action daily.

Involve others.
- Ask: "Is my Action Plan realistic, specific, and limited in scope?"

- Publicly commit to making personal changes in how you handle conflict.

View your organization as a supportive partner in your endeavor to change.
- Seek out on-the-job opportunities to improve, such as volunteering to chair a committee.

- Investigate what organizational resources will help you, for example, human resources staff or books and manuals on conflict resolution.

- Remember that good things come to those who change — promotions, raises, a solid reputation, and new opportunities.

Conflict Dynamics Action Plan: Potential Obstacles

Anticipate barriers, setbacks, and needs.
- What personal and professional obstacles might hinder my progress?

- How will I overcome obstacles?

- What organizational resources will I need (money for seminar training or books, time from others for feedback, etc.)?

When obstacles arise or setbacks occur, I vow to:
- Persist, persevere, and progress.

- Use what I have learned so far to go even farther.

- Remember: Continual progress is a continuous process.

_____

_____

_____

_____

_____

_____

_____

_____

_____

_____

_____

Conflict Dynamics Action Plan: Measuring Progress

Keep a logbook or journal to track progress. Frequently evaluate:
- How am I doing?

- What have I learned?

- Have my goals been realistic and sufficiently limited in scope?

- If I have not been making progress, why not?

- Do I need to adjust my Action Plan?

Seek feedback from others. Select from among those individuals who:
- Have multiple opportunities to observe you in conflict situations.

- Will be honest and direct with you.

- Will give advice as well as encouragement and support.

- Will hold you to your commitment to change.

In your feedback sessions with others:
- Thank them for their time and for providing you with feedback.

- Emphasize that you value their honesty, observations, and advice.

- As you listen, take notes.

- Don't get defensive or angry. Stay open-minded.

- Re-affirm your public commitment for personal change.

- Enlist their continued support.

Reward yourself for progress.
- Congratulate yourself for small successes. (Remember, the more limited and specific your goals, the more frequently you'll achieve small successes.)

- Treat yourself in a special way for reaching bigger milestones.

Conflict Dynamics Action Plan: Target Date

Recognize that:
- The time it takes to achieve goals varies by individual. What takes one person six months may take someone else a year.

- Unless it is an extremely simple goal, it will be difficult and require considerable time, effort, and perseverance.

- Stumbling blocks are likely to occur. Expect the unexpected and keep going.

When setting your Target Dates:
- Keep your time frames specific, limited, and realistic (just like your goals).

- Factor in extra time for unanticipated events and obstacles.

- When publicly committing to your goals for personal change, include your Target Dates.

- Pledge to do some goal-oriented action daily.

If you don't achieve your goal by your Target Date, evaluate what happened (or didn't happen) and why.
- Were you unrealistic in setting your goal or Target Date?

- Did you try to do too much too soon?

- Did unanticipated obstacles arise?

- Did you lack others' support or necessary resources?

- What insights do others have?

_____

_____

_____

_____

_____

_____

_____

_____

_____

_____

_____

_____

In setting a new Target Date:
- *Don't* be discouraged. *Don't* beat yourself up. Take a deep breath and try again.

- Consider establishing a smaller, interim goal or "sub-goal." Keep it very specific and very limited.

- Double or triple the amount of time you anticipate this will require.

- Seek input from others as you revise your plan.

- Remember that what's most important is that you change, not how long it takes you to do so.

Motto: Continuous process, continual progress.

CDP Developmental Worksheet: Responses to Conflict

conflict dynamics profile®

	Self			Boss			Peers			Direct Reports		
	Actual Score	Area of Strength	Development Opportunity	Actual Score	Area of Strength	Development Opportunity	Actual Score	Area of Strength	Development Opportunity	Actual Score	Area of Strength	Development Opportunity
		> 55	< 45		> 55	< 45		> 55	< 45		> 55	< 45
Active-Constructive Responses												
Perspective Taking												
Creating Solutions												
Expressing Emotions												
Reaching Out												
Passive-Constructive Responses												
Reflective Thinking												
Delay Responding												
Adapting												
		< 45	> 55		< 45	> 55		< 45	> 55		< 45	> 55
Active-Destructive Responses												
Winning												
Displaying Anger												
Demeaning Others												
Retaliating												
Passive-Destructive Responses												
Avoiding												
Yielding												
Hiding Emotions												
Self-Criticizing												

Highest Priority to Develop:

1. _____
2. _____
3. _____

11

Hot Buttons

Hot Buttons, those situations and individuals that you find most annoying, can provoke and escalate conflict. By learning about the situations in which you are most likely to feel upset, you can better avoid conflicts in the future. By understanding and examining the links between provocation and response, you can better control your behavior.

Indicate below each of your Hot Button scores. Then, for the three Hot Buttons with the highest scores, rank-order their "Importance of Cooling," taking into consideration the following factors:

• Your level of frustration and irritation (that is, your score).

• How frequently this Hot Button provokes you into conflict.

• The degree to which provocation of this Hot Button interferes with your job performance.

• The degree to which provocation of this Hot Button interferes with your physical and emotional well-being.

The Hot Button ranked Number 1 should be the Hot Button that you most want (or need) to change.

Hot Button	Your Score	Importance of Cooling
Unreliable	_____	_____
Overly Analytical	_____	_____
Unappreciative	_____	_____
Aloof	_____	_____
Micro-Managing	_____	_____
Self-Centered	_____	_____
Abrasive	_____	_____
Untrustworthy	_____	_____
Hostile	_____	_____

Notes

_____   _____
_____   _____
_____   _____
_____   _____
_____   _____
_____   _____
_____   _____
_____   _____
_____   _____
_____   _____
_____   _____
_____   _____
_____   _____
_____   _____
_____   _____
_____   _____
_____   _____
_____   _____
_____   _____
_____   _____
_____   _____
_____   _____
_____   _____
_____   _____
_____   _____
_____   _____
_____   _____

CONFLICT DYNAMICS ACTION PLAN: SAMPLE

DYNAMIC GOAL: *To take action by being more assertive*

Constructive action to take:	Potential obstacles:	Measure progress by:	Target Date:
1. Make public commitment to be more assertive	None	Feedback from Beth	2 months
2. Communicate openly to Boss about resolving conflict	1. Boss is avoiding-type 2. My hostile Hot Button	Meeting(s) with Boss	1 month

DYNAMIC GOAL: *To focus on what I do well and stop Self-Criticizing*

Constructive action to take:	Potential obstacles:	Measure progress by:	Target Date:
1. Keep diary of negative thoughts	Anxious about upcoming annual review	Weekly review of diary (fewer negative thoughts)	3 months
2. Think good thoughts and be optimistic	Boss is abrasive and critical	1. Support from team members 2. Weekly review of diary (more positive thoughts)	3 months
3. Remember: QTIP — Quit Taking It Personally!	None	Reciting frequently each day	Immediately

CONFLICT DYNAMICS ACTION PLAN

DYNAMIC GOAL: _____

Constructive action to take:

Potential obstacles:

Measure progress by:

Target Date:

DYNAMIC GOAL: _____

Constructive action to take:

Potential obstacles:

Measure progress by:

Target Date:

CONFLICT DYNAMICS ACTION PLAN

DYNAMIC GOAL: _____

Constructive action to take:	**Potential obstacles:**	**Measure progress by:**	**Target Date:**

DYNAMIC GOAL: _____

Constructive action to take:	**Potential obstacles:**	**Measure progress by:**	**Target Date:**

CONFLICT DYNAMICS ACTION PLAN

DYNAMIC GOAL: _____

Constructive action to take:

Potential obstacles:

Measure progress by:

Target Date:

DYNAMIC GOAL: _____

Constructive action to take:

Potential obstacles:

Measure progress by:

Target Date:

Notes

Notes

Notes

Chapter III

Confronting Conflict Constructively

If you don't scale the mountain, you can't see the view.

Anonymous

At this point in your life, you probably react to conflict in habitual ways. Perhaps you get angry regardless of the size or severity of the issue. Maybe you go to great lengths to avoid confrontation and have since childhood. Or possibly, even though you vow that you'll not be pushed around next time, the status quo prevails. What you want to learn is to respond to conflict in purposeful and productive ways. Rather than reacting automatically in a manner that prolongs or escalates conflict, you want to resolve conflicts constructively. This section focuses on that goal and describes in detail new ways to think, feel, and act when confronted with conflict.

Lessons in Conflict

Before learning constructive methods of responding to conflict, a few initial lessons are in order. These five lessons represent themes that are repeated throughout ***Managing Conflict Dynamics*** and are a good starting point for changing how you view conflict and conflict resolution.

Lesson #1: You are not alone. You will find that other people are willing, even eager, to assist you because by helping you, they're helping themselves. If you can learn to manage conflict more constructively, their lives and work environment will be filled with greater understanding and collaboration and less tension and anger. Ask others for feedback. Use as role models those who handle conflict successfully.

Lesson #2: Responses to conflict are learned. Responses to conflict, that is, the emotions you feel and the behaviors you enact, are learned. You've learned them through years of personal experience. You've been taught by your parents, siblings, teachers, friends, and mentors. You've been influenced by your society's culture via books, movies, television, political leaders, sports heroes, and other role models. Through all this, you've learned beneficial as well as ineffective and harmful methods of managing and resolving conflict. But just as you have learned destructive methods of managing and resolving conflict, you can learn new constructive ones.

Lesson #3: You control how you feel and respond. You control your emotions; they don't control you. You control your behavior; it doesn't control you. If, for example, you express your anger by ranting and raving, that's your choice. If you hold your anger inside, that's your choice as well. You have control. You have choices. You can change.

Lesson #4: You can affect the direction and intensity of a conflict. Research on conflict reveals two key ways to do this. First, destructive behaviors such as displaying anger and retaliating, are disproportionately important in affecting how a conflict may unfold. Therefore, it is generally more important to avoid negative, exacerbating responses than it is to engage in the "soothing," constructive ones. Second, actions and events that take place early can have a huge impact on later events and actions. Thus, in a conflict's earliest stages, responding constructively (or at least not harmfully) will be more effective than actions taken later on. In other words, act early and do no harm.

Lesson #5: Conflict resolution is dynamic. Conflict resolution, like conflict, is a dynamic process. It requires give and take, learning and understanding, listening and communicating, thought and action. It necessitates recognizing how emotions, words, and deeds (yours and theirs) affect what's happening, or what's not happening. In a general sense, conflict resolution involves getting your needs met while meeting the needs of other people. Your needs must be on the table, and your task is to find out what the other person might need. Doing this will require all of the methods of confronting conflict that comprise ***Managing Conflict Dynamics: A Practical Approach***.

Confronting Conflict Constructively

All of the techniques described here are constructive ways of responding to conflict. Some of these strategies are more active, others more passive. The description of each technique begins with a thought-provoking quotation and an example of a destructive way of handling conflict. This is then followed by a discussion of more constructive ways of responding and the advantages of doing so. Finally, detailed and specific advice is provided which, when combined with determination and effort, will enable you to confront conflict constructively.

Table 4: The Keys to Confronting Conflict Constructively outlines the organization of this section and could even serve as a "short course" in conflict management. The four main headings follow a general sequence for successful conflict resolution.

Table 4: The Keys to Confronting Conflict Constructively

BUILDING RELATIONSHIPS

- *Dynamic Listening:*
  Perspective Taking, Understanding, Patience, Open-mindedness, Being Attentive

- *Dynamic Communication:*
  Reflective Thinking, Dynamic Listening, Developing Rapport, Honesty, Strategic Silence

- *Criticizing Constructively:*
  Praising, Focusing on Performance, Sensitivity, Tact, Being Non-judgmental

MANAGING EMOTIONS

- *Taking Time Outs:*
  Getting Distance, Delay Responding, Controlling Emotions, Re-focusing

- *Controlling Anger:*
  Calming Down, Expressing Anger Appropriately, Criticizing Constructively

- *Reaching Out:*
  Repairing Emotions, Making Amends, Dynamic Listening, Dynamic Communication

- *Expressing Emotions:*
  Dynamic Communication, Honesty, Being Informative and Appropriate

RESOLVING CONFLICT

- *Taking Action:*
  Staying Involved, Moving Forward, Overcoming Fears, Persistence, Assertiveness

- *Cooperating:*
  Flexibility, Reciprocity, Non-competitiveness, Winning for Everyone

- *Dynamic Conflict Resolution:*
  Creating Solutions, Collaborating, Dynamic Listening, Dynamic Communication

ACCEPTING CONFLICT

- *Self-Appraisal:*
  Evaluating Self, Seeking Perspective, Being Realistic and Confident

- *Adapting:*
  Coping, Accepting, Optimism, Flexibility, Integrity

- *When Conflicts Can't be Resolved:*
  Evaluating Career and Well-Being, Contemplating Alternatives, Weighing Options

Building Relationships

One important component to managing conflict successfully is building and maintaining satisfactory work and social relationships. Obviously, relationships built on trust, concern, and appreciation will be better able to withstand the turmoil of conflict. But even during or after a conflict, relationships can be enhanced depending upon your skills. With regard to workplace conflict, the most important relationship-building skills concern communication: how we listen to others and how we deliver information to them.

This section examines three communication-related aspects of relationship building that are vital to the process of conflict management. **Dynamic Listening** is an active process, one that requires patience, perspective taking, and understanding. **Dynamic Communication** is comprised of reflective thinking, rapport, and an open and honest exchange of information. **Criticizing Constructively** requires sensitivity as one balances criticism and appreciation. What these topics have in common is consideration of and attention to the person with whom one is in conflict.

Top Tips For Building Relationships

1. Treat everyone as a client — with respect, courtesy, concern and appreciation.

2. Foster an atmosphere of open communication and accessibility.

3. Listen more than you talk.

4. Show you CARE: Compliment, Appreciate, Reward, Encourage.

5. Value differences and diversity.

DYNAMIC LISTENING

Know how to listen, and you will profit even from those who talk badly.

Plutarch

Dynamic Example:

Bob approached his boss expecting to resolve easily a minor concern he had over his new responsibilities. Andrea, after all, was very easy to talk with, interested in what others had to say, and understanding of her employees' needs. Today, however, had been a long, hard day, and Andrea was focused on paperwork when Bob entered her office. He'd barely begun to speak when Andrea, without even looking up, interrupted: "Your concerns are ridiculous. You can do this. Good night."

The secret to being a good listener is to listen in the manner that you want to be listened to when it's your turn to speak. That means being attentive, patient, and working to understand the "who, what, why and how" of the message being expressed. In the midst of a conflict, the last thing you may feel like doing is listening, but if you can do so patiently and open-mindedly, then the more likely it is that you will be listened to when it's your turn to speak.

Listening is a *process* that combines patience, attention to details, and open-mindedness. It requires the listener to probe, ask questions, and repeatedly urge the other person to "Tell me more." It requires restating and paraphrasing what the other said in order to ensure that what the listener heard is really what the speaker meant. Listening, then, is not merely hearing but understanding.

An essential component of understanding, and therefore a key to conflict resolution, is perspective taking. Like listening, perspective taking is an active process, one that involves putting one's self in the other person's place and imagining what that person is thinking or feeling. Understanding another's point of view paves the way for such constructive means of conflict resolution as criticizing constructively, taking action, cooperating, creating solutions, and repairing emotions.

Active listening and perspective taking require time and energy, and you may feel tempted to hurry the process along. The consequences of doing so, however, can be costly: overlooked information, lost time due to confusion and misunderstandings, neglected interpersonal relationships, and missed opportunities to resolve conflict. Because of the positive repercussions for interpersonal relationships and conflict resolution, as well as for you and your organization, the time and effort required for Dynamic Listening are well worth it.

Before Conflict

Begin with Reflection Questions.
- Do I listen with my eyes as well as my ears?

- Does this conflict signal issues I have neglected or problems I have overlooked?

- What cues indicated that conflict was about to erupt?

- What have been the personal and professional consequences of not listening?

- How do I want to be viewed when the conflict is over?

_____
_____
_____
_____
_____
_____
_____
_____
_____
_____
_____
_____
_____
_____

From the other person's point of view, examine your own approach to conflict and conflict resolution.

- What are the weaknesses in my approach?

- How would I attack my own position or attempts at resolution?

- What motivates the other person against me?

- Do I really understand what the other person wants?

- What does the other person think I want?

- What does the other person really need to have?

_____
_____
_____
_____
_____

_____
_____
_____
_____
_____
_____
_____

Practice perspective taking by pretending you are not you. Select a person quite different from you or one who has a different point of view. Answer the following questions as you think this person would:

- What information or experiences have influenced "your" perspective?

- How does "your" thinking affect "your" behavior?

- What motivates "you"?

- How do "you" typically react when faced with conflict, and why?

- By what means do "you" try to resolve conflict resolution, and why?

_____
_____
_____
_____
_____
_____
_____
_____
_____
_____
_____
_____

Tell yourself:
- I will listen with my ears, eyes, body, and mind.

- Be patient, open-minded, and willing to change.

- Search for mutual interests, needs, problems, and goals.

- I will respect others' perceptions of me and my behavior as valid. Their views are reality for them and they will act accordingly.

During Conflict

Be attentive and supportive.
- Give the speaker your full and undivided attention.

- Show attentiveness and receptivity by sitting up straight and leaning slightly forward. Don't cross your arms over your chest.

- Backchannel, that is, signal that you're listening by nodding your head or saying "I see." This does not mean you must agree.

- Even if receiving negative information or feedback, remain open-minded.

- Let the speaker finish. *Never interrupt.*

Listen with your eyes.
- Maintain good eye contact (but don't stare).

- Observe the speaker's eyes and face. The mouth, eyebrows, and forehead are especially revealing of emotional states.

- Observe the speaker's body language.

Shift perspectives.
- Mentally put yourself in the other's place

and work to understand his/her point of view, motivation, reaction to the conflict, and approach to conflict resolution.

- Focus on the other's words and behavior, rather than your assumptions.

- Reframe "That's a ridiculous point of view" to "I wonder why s/he thinks that."

Do not assume that you know how the other person thinks or feels.
- Establish an atmosphere of open communication.

- Encourage the other person to talk or vent.

- Ask open-ended questions.

- Empathize and let the other know when you understand and when you don't.

- Be sure you know what the person needs.

Make certain you understood the other person's position.
- Rephrase, restate, or summarize what you think has been said.

- Ask for examples to clarify the issues.

- Solicit ideas and solutions.

- Take responsibility for not understanding.

- Acknowledge the other's position without agreeing with it by saying "That's an interesting point of view" or "Many people have that same position."

If you find yourself angry or if you need time to engage in perspective taking, delay responding (see Taking Time Outs, Page 39).
- Take a deep breath and slowly count to 10.

- Request a time-out.

- Do not respond until you feel ready to continue.

After Conflict

Assess yourself.
- What did I do well?

- What areas still need improvement?

- In what ways did perspective taking aid the process?

- How will others view me and my actions?

- If the conflict remains, is it due to a lack of listening or perspective taking on my part?

_____

_____

_____

_____

_____

_____

_____

_____

_____

Seek feedback from trusted others.
- Was I attentive to verbal and non-verbal cues?

- Did I work to understand the other person's position?

- Was I accurate in my perspective taking?

_____

_____

_____

_____

_____

_____

_____

_____

Engage in perspective taking.
- How is the other person feeling now?

- If I were in this person's shoes, how would I want others to respond to me?

_____

_____

_____

_____

_____

_____

_____

_____

_____

_____

_____

_____

Follow up with the person with whom you were in conflict.
- Ask: "Did I understand everything you were trying to express?"

- Get to know the person better. This will make perspective taking easier in the future.

Motto:
When I listen,
people talk.

DYNAMIC COMMUNICATION

*Be not careless in deeds, nor
confused in words, nor rambling
in thoughts.*

Marcus Aurelius

Dynamic Example:

Scott's anxiety in conflict situations typically led him to interrupt others and to respond impulsively. Today was no exception. Before Barbara even finished presenting her marketing plan, Scott blurted out that his plan was better. An open debate began on the merits of each, but Scott was so emphatic in his opinions, that Barbara and several others felt uncomfortable and completely stifled. Oblivious to it all, Scott continued to argue. Barbara noted to herself that this was his pattern — react first, reflect later.

During conflict, it is important to communicate in a way that constructively moves you along the path to conflict resolution. The first step in that journey is listening attentively while withholding judgement. The second is responding in the same manner, that is, explaining your position through thoughtfully-chosen words and actions, while monitoring the other person's perspective and reactions. As with listening, communication is *dynamic* because of the attentiveness and continuous, sometimes subtle, interaction required between the parties as they work to resolve their conflict.

The first step in dynamic communication is reflective thinking. Reflective thinking means taking time to analyze the situation and consider alternative ways of responding.

Reflective thinking is useful at all stages of a conflict. It allows one time to view the conflict from a variety of angles, to take the perspective of the other person, and to repair emotions if they were damaged. In addition, the time can be used to organize one's thoughts and plans, create solutions, and make well-thought-out decisions.

The second step in dynamic communication is responding in a manner that constructively moves you towards conflict resolution. That means developing rapport, speaking directly and honestly without being hurtful, encouraging the expression of differing viewpoints, and most importantly, exchanging information about needs. Understanding your needs as well as the other person's is critical to resolving conflicts and building solid relationships. During conflict, it can be difficult to keep the lines of communication open, but it is absolutely necessary, for without communication, there will be no conflict resolution.

Clearly, being impulsive, anxious, or trying to hurry the process along can result in being perceived as a poor listener, a poor decision-maker, or as an insensitive or bombastic person. Dynamic communication requires patience — the patience to listen with both eyes and ears, the patience to think before speaking, and patience while drawing out the other person. But only by taking the time and making the effort can you achieve the constructive dialogue that results in mutually satisfactory conflict resolution.

Before Conflict

Begin with Reflection Questions.
- Do I work to keep the lines of communication open?

- Am I attentive to nonverbal communication (my own and others')?

- What have been the personal and professional consequences of not responding in a sensitive manner?

- In which past conflicts would reflective thinking have been useful? How?

- Do I let others know what I need? Am I aware of others' needs?

- How do I want to be viewed when the conflict is over?

_____

_____

_____

_____

_____

_____

_____

_____

_____

_____

_____

_____

Practice taking time to think *before* reacting. Pick a day in which before you act on any request, make a judgement, or do anything, you will:
- First, note your initial reaction.

- Then, carefully consider alternative reactions and others' points-of-view, and the pros and cons of each.

- Analyze why your first reaction occurred first. Because it was the right decision? Or "the way it's always been done"? Were you in a hurry or perhaps over-anxious?

_____

_____

_____

_____

_____

_____

_____

_____

_____

_____

_____

_____

_____

_____

_____

_____

Develop ways to avoid communication breakdowns.
- Hold informal get-togethers that have no agenda.

- Share information and encourage your co-workers to do likewise.

- Promptly return phone messages and reply to correspondence.

Tell yourself:
- TLC — Think, Listen, Communicate.

- Be calm, clear, and in control of my words and actions.

- I want to resolve the conflict and maintain a good relationship.

During Conflict

Establish rules for handling conflicts openly.
- Remain respectful.

- Try to appreciate differences in style and opinions.

- Profanity, name-calling, shouting, and violence (threatened or actual) are prohibited.

Encourage open communication.
- Lead the way. Express yourself openly and sincerely.

- Share your goal: a thoughtful, frank, and constructive dialogue.

- Don't lead with your opinions.

- Encourage the other person to freely express him/herself.

- Solicit input from other parties (if appropriate) and allow them to raise issues.

- Be humble. "Whenever you're wrong, admit it; whenever you're right, shut up" (Ogden Nash).

Without listening, there can be no communication. Employ Dynamic Listening (Page 25), especially these points:
- Be attentive and supportive.

- Ask questions to help clarify.

- Allow others to finish speaking — *never interrupt*.

- Engage in perspective taking to understand others' points of view.

Make your points in a non-threatening way.
- Speak clearly. Be direct and brief.

- Use the other party's name whenever possible.

- Use terms others can understand.

Define terms when necessary.
- *Never* express prejudice, hostility, arrogance, or disinterest.

- Depersonalize the conflict. Attack problems, not people.

- Preface your opinions or suggestions with "Perhaps" or "One possible approach is. . . ."

Be assertive, not aggressive, in your non-verbal communication.
- Maintain steady eye contact (but don't stare).

- Lean slightly forward. Have a relaxed posture but don't sway or slouch.

- Speak firmly and with a moderate rate of speech.

- Shouting, finger-jabbing, an angry expression or tone of voice will be interpreted as aggression and will serve to escalate conflict.

Silence can be golden. Strategic or tactical silence allows you to:
- Observe the other person in order to understand his/her perspective.

- Organize your thoughts and strategies.

- Contemplate what has been discussed and what will be following. The longer the pause, the more dramatic will be the impact of what follows.

- Express yourself non-verbally.

- Detach yourself from emotions of the moment. Cool down before you speak up.

Stop frequently to make sure the other person understands you.
- Ask the other to paraphrase what s/he believes you said.

- Ask for ideas and solutions.

- Encourage continual participation and dialogue from the other person.

- Reward understanding by saying "Exactly!" or "You're right. That's what was I trying to say."

Look for signs of others' resistance to your response.
- Avoiding eye contact.

- Leaning back with arms crossed or a tense posture.

- Being especially argumentative or quiet.

- Appearing disinterested, distracted, or emotional.

While humor can be a wonderful icebreaker, it can also backfire or be misinterpreted. In trying to address conflict with humor, *be very careful.*
- First rule of comedy: timing is everything. Pick your moment.

- Know your audience. Be sure they will get the joke.

- Absolutely no humor that could be construed as sexist, racist, homophobic, etc.

- Absolutely no sarcasm or cynicism.

- A joke aimed at yourself is usually less risky than a joke aimed at someone else.

If you need time to think or cool down:
- Remind yourself: "I control my emotions; they don't control me."

- Delay responding by requesting a time-out, leaving the room, or counting to 10. See also Taking Time Outs (Page 39) and Controlling Anger (Page 43).

Just as you need time for reflective thinking, so do others. Give them time to:
- Digest new information and ideas.

- Create solutions.

- Make decisions.

- Respond in a thoughtful manner.

If you must be negative in your response, be careful and considerate. Review Criticizing Constructively (Page 34), especially these rules:
- Attack the problem, not the person.

- Balance negative statements with compliments and appreciation for things done well.

- Avoid accusations or any suggestions of blame.

- Use "I" rather than "You."

After Conflict

Assess yourself.
- What did I do well?

- What areas still need improvement?

- Are changes necessary in the decisions I made during conflict?

- Was I attentive and sensitive to the other party's cues and needs?

- How did I use my reflective thinking time?

- How will others view me and my actions?

- If the conflict remains, is it due to a lack of reflective thinking or communicating on my part?

_____

_____

_____

_____

_____

_____

_____

_____

_____

_____

_____

_____

_____

_____

_____

_____

Seek feedback from trusted others.
- Did I respond appropriately and sensitively?

- Did I express myself in a clear, non-aggressive manner?

- Was I impulsive in my words or behavior?

- Did I encourage and reward openly expressed thoughts and feelings?

_____

_____

_____

_____

_____

_____

_____

_____

_____

_____

_____

Follow up with the person with whom you were in conflict.
- Continue to keep the lines of communication open.

- If you responded angrily or inappropriately:

  - Apologize.

  - Make every effort to get the relationship back on track. This may even require the involvement of a third party to serve as a go-between.

If the conflict remains unresolved or emotions continue to run high, it may be best to respond to the conflict in writing rather than face-to-face.
- Write in the manner you would be speaking: clear, concise, non-emotional, professional.

- Explain that you are writing rather than speaking face-to-face because this is an issue about which there are strong feelings, and you want to ensure the maximum amount of understanding.

- Keep your writing focused on the issues of the conflict and not the personalities of the parties involved.

Motto:
T L C –
Think, Listen, Communicate.

CRITICIZING CONSTRUCTIVELY

The rule in carving holds good to criticism; never cut with a knife what you can cut with a spoon.
                    Charles Buxton

Dynamic Example:

Steve was excited about his presentation to the department, but a bit anxious about the presence of Kathleen. Usually, no matter who was presenting or what was said, Kathleen expressed her disagreement by sighing loudly, making faces, and interrupting with sarcastic comments. Despite his determination not to let her bother him this time, Steve lost his focus when Kathleen began sifting through papers and rolling her eyes. He rushed through his presentation and, in doing so, skipped a crucial graph. Kathleen's way of pointing this out was to ask whether Steve had "prepared randomly or just not at all." Steve, who could have spent more time in preparation, felt humiliated and angry.

One common response during conflict is to demean the other person, perhaps by responding with sarcasm, ridiculing behavior, or destructive criticism. The effect of this, no matter how unintended it might be, is frequently to increase the anger and hostility that others feel. This, in turn, makes it difficult to keep conflicts from escalating into increasingly intense disagreements.

The function of criticism is to convey information about one's standards and expectations. Through constructive criticism, one sensitively expresses exactly what the other person must do in order to reach, or even exceed, personal or organizational expecta-

tions. Criticism that is expressed constructively and sensitively can produce the desired changes while maintaining good relationships and dampening conflict

Even constructive criticism, however, can lead to conflict and hard feelings. One way this occurs concerns the manner in which the criticism is delivered. No matter how well-chosen one's words of criticism, the message will be undercut by a sneering tone of voice, the rolling of one's eyes, or a smirk. Demeaning behaviors are hurtful, so much so that the information one is trying to convey regarding standards and expectations can be lost. In short, the style of delivering criticism is at least as important as the substance.

A second way in which criticism can lead to conflict occurs when one is criticized to the exclusion of positive reinforcement. No matter how well-intentioned such criticism might be, its unrelenting nature can make the target feel his/her work is never good enough and that the standards are simply impossible to attain. Without praise or "strokes" to counterbalance the continual criticism, the target will be convinced that no matter how conscientiously one might work, all efforts will be judged as substandard. Therefore, why work hard? The criticism will be forthcoming regardless. Consequently, the work is indeed substandard, the workers are frustrated, angry and demoralized, and ultimately, the organization suffers.

Criticism that is destructive, unrelenting, or delivered in a demeaning manner must be managed so as to counteract the negative emotions and conflict that can result. Constructive criticism requires that specific rather than general information regarding standards and expectations be expressed via well-chosen, non-hurtful words *and* behavior, and that criticism be balanced with praise.

Before Conflict

Begin with Reflection Questions.

- Is my criticism directed at the behavior and *not* the person?

- When I deliver critical comments to another person, am I aware of my facial gestures and body language?

- Do I provide enough praise for a job well done?

- Are my standards concerning deadlines and quality of work reasonable and attainable given the nature of my co-workers?

- Am I critical in front of other people?

- Before criticizing, do I consider how sensitive the other person might be or the reaction I may invoke?

- What have been the personal and professional consequences of demeaning or harshly criticizing others?

- How do I want to be viewed when the conflict is over?

_____

_____

_____

_____

_____

_____

_____

Constructive criticism:

- Begins with "I" rather than "You." For example, "Can't you spell?" is accusatory and likely to put the other person on the defensive. Instead say, "I am disappointed at the number of typos in this report."

- Focuses on the person's work performance rather than his or her personality. For example, change "You're so lazy" to "This report is missing an important section."

- Is specific regarding expectations and standards, for instance, "I am unable to accept this work because it arrived after the deadline."

- Balances criticism with praise, for example, "You have shown a lot of initiative. Now what's needed is more detail and focus."

Practice changing destructive criticism into constructive criticism.

- Write down instances of harsh or demeaning comments that you have either made or heard others make.

- Take the perspective of the target of those comments. How did s/he feel after hearing them?

- Re-write the destructive criticism style that is non-hurtful yet informative.

- Again, take the target's perspective. How would s/he be likely to feel this time?

- Practice aloud examples of constructive criticism.

_____

_____

_____

_____

_____

_____

Think thoughts that are non-judgmental.
- He's not incompetent or stupid, he just approaches things differently than I do.
- Her point-of-view may be based on information I don't have.
- Change "I am better than you" to "We are both important."

Tell yourself:
- My goal is to inform and encourage, not hurt or demoralize.
- I will think before speaking.
- Constructive criticism curbs conflict.

During Conflict

Express your criticism tactfully, sensitively, and privately.
- Emphasize that your goal is not personal but professional — to improve the organization's functioning and environment.
- Share with the other person some of your own mistakes.
- The more specific the criticism, the more useful it will be and the easier to address.
- Balance negative statements with compliments and appreciation for things done well.
- If appropriate, offer to help the person improve. Express your willingness to assist in developing an action plan or to serve as a coach or role model.

Attack the problem, not the person.
- Focus on the situation, ideas and problem solving rather than personal characteristics or failings.
- Emphasize facts rather than judgements.

- Shouting, name-calling, blame, profanity, etc. will escalate conflict and tension.
- Be respectful and polite. Express appreciation for differing opinions and approaches.
- Absolutely no sarcasm or cynical remarks.

Employ Dynamic Communication (Page 29), especially these points:
- Be aware of your non-verbal language, especially tone of voice and facial expression.
- Stop frequently to make sure the other person understands what you are saying.
- Use the other party's name whenever possible.

Demeaning behavior and destructive criticism often have their roots in anger. Review Controlling Anger (Page 43), especially these points:
- Remind yourself that emotions are learned responses that you control.
- Delay responding in order to maintain your composure.
- Explain clearly and calmly why you are angry.

If you feel the urge to make a destructive or demeaning remark, STOP!
- Reflect on the likely reaction and consequences of acting on your urge.
- Say something positive. Remind yourself that it costs you nothing to do so yet the rewards can be plentiful.
- If you can't say anything positive, say nothing.

If necessary to soothe hurt feelings, try Reaching Out (Page 47), especially these points:

- Acknowledge his/her emotions.

- Provide time for the person to compose him/herself.

- Admit your responsibility and apologize.

After Conflict

Assess yourself.
- What did I do well?

- What areas still need improvement?

- Did I make the criticism a win-win situation for both parties?

- How will others view me and my actions?

- If the conflict remains, is it due to my destructive criticism or demeaning others?

_____

_____

_____

_____

_____

_____

_____

_____

_____

_____

Seek feedback from trusted others.
- Was my criticism constructive, reasonable, and attainable?

- Did my facial gestures and body language undercut what I said?

- Were my comments equitable and not biased towards any group of people?

_____

_____

_____

_____

_____

_____

_____

Follow up with the person with whom you were in conflict.
- Ensure that your criticism was:

  - Taken to be constructive.

  - Aimed at developing the person.

  - About the person's performance rather than personality.

- Establish that your relationship remains friendly and professional.

  - Compliment the person or otherwise boost his/her self-esteem.

  - If appropriate, express your willingness to help the person improve.

- If your efforts at changing the other's behavior seem to be successful:

  - Praise every improvement, no matter how small.

  - Emphasize the benefits of continuing to change.

Motto:
Constructive criticism
curbs conflict.

Managing Emotions

Perhaps the most difficult part of managing conflict is handling the powerful emotions which conflict often produces. In some cases, it will be your own emotions that need managing — your feelings of anger, frustration, resentment, or anxiety. Allowing these emotions to get the better of you can turn a relatively minor conflict into a serious one very quickly. At other times, however, it will be the emotions of other people that are most relevant. Helping others effectively cope with their strong feelings can be crucial to resolving conflict satisfactorily and maintaining good working relationships.

Examined in this section are four aspects of managing emotions. *Taking Time Outs* describes techniques for controlling emotions and delaying your first impulse; this provides you (and others) with the time necessary to re-focus on the problems at hand. *Controlling Anger* emphasizes managing one's anger so that it can be expressed in suitable and appropriate ways. Repairing emotions and making amends are components of *Reaching Out*, a process as important for building relationships as it is for resolving conflicts. *Expressing Emotions* concerns those feelings that, when hidden, can be detrimental to the process of conflict resolution. Being calm, honest, informative, and appropriate are the keys to managing emotions.

Top Tips For Managing Emotions

1. Provide Triple A emotional services: Anticipate, Acknowledge, Apologize.

2. Chill out with time out.

3. Control your emotions; don't let them control you.

4. The choice is yours. Choose to feel differently.

5. Channel your emotional energy in constructive directions.

TAKING TIME OUTS

*What is time but the stuff delay
is made of?*
Henry David Thoreau

Dynamic Example:

Diane's frustration at the slow pace of the labor-management negotiations was taking its toll. Her fidgeting eventually turned to distress at the amount of time being wasted and the unfinished project back on her desk. Her actions and emotions did not go unnoticed by one of the lead attorneys, who turned his attention to her and asked for her contribution to the discussion. Instead of being able to discuss her idea for resolving the impasse, all Diane could express was her irritation at the proceedings. An embarrassed and awkward silence ensued. Someone called for a time out but it was too late to help Diane. Her reputation had already been damaged, and her boss made a mental note to exclude Diane from further meetings.

A common occurrence during conflict is for individuals to become so upset by the situation that they begin to act in rash and emotional ways. Therefore, a constructive way to respond to conflict is to establish some psychological and possibly even physical distance from the conflict by taking a "time out" and letting things settle down. This could involve withholding an immediate response when provoked, temporarily leaving the situation, or turning to other issues for a while and coming back to the conflict later.

Calling a time out when faced with a conflict or tense situation gives people the time necessary to distance themselves emotionally from the conflict and re-focus on conflict resolution. Time out does *not* mean opt out, cop out, back out, or drop out. Rather, a time out allows you to control the emotions that are created as well as inhibit an initial, perhaps destructive, reaction or a poor decision.

Two factors help make time out a successful way to manage emotions. The first one is taking enough time to calm down. Research on the physiology of stress indicates that most people require 20 minutes to calm down (that's how long it takes for one's heart rate to return to normal). Re-entering an emotional or stressful situation while still physiologically aroused will defeat the purpose of the time out. Second, regardless of where you go or what you do, the real secret to calming down is what you tell yourself during the time out. Stressful, irritated, angry thoughts will only exacerbate your stress, irritation, and anger. Peaceful, tranquil, conflict-resolving thoughts will promote calmness and constructive ideas for conflict resolution.

Before Conflict

Begin with Reflection Questions.
* In which past conflicts would time outs have been beneficial?
* How would I as well as others have benefited from using time outs in past conflicts?
* What have been the personal and professional consequences of not taking timeouts or not delaying my first response?
* How do I want to be viewed when the conflict is over?

_____

_____

_____

_____

_____

_____

_____

_____

_____

_____

Practice a deep breathing technique.
- From your diaphragm (not chest) inhale slowly and deeply.

- As you inhale, think "Calm."

- From your diaphragm, exhale as slowly as you inhaled.

- As you exhale, think "Peace."

- Repeat the process two more times.

Practice saying: "I want to take a time out." Be prepared to act on this.

Decide upon the method(s) of time out to use when you are unable to physically leave the situation, for example:
- Change the subject to something less emotional.

- Slowly count to 10 or 20 (or higher if necessary).

- Take a "mental trip." Envision a peaceful, calm setting such as a beach or mountain stream. Imagine that you are really there and away from all conflict and tension.

Decide upon the method(s) of time out to use if you are able to leave the situation for a short while, for example:
- Do something physical, such as walk around the building or jog in a secluded hallway.

- Listen to music.

- Peruse a book of inspirational quotations or other favorite book.

- Leaf through a file of cartoons and comic strips that you keep for an occasion such as this.

Decide upon the method(s) to use if you need an extended time out, for example:
- Put a sign on your office door such as "In a meeting," "Do not disturb," or even "In Time Out!"

- Read something calming, inspirational, and completely unrelated to the job.

- Get out of the workplace for a few hours.

Encourage your organization or department to:
- Institute a company-wide signal that will indicate to everyone when a person is in time out and should not be disturbed (e.g., an "In Time Out" door hanger for each office).

- Designate a "Time Out Place" or "Quiet Room" where people can go to calm down. Decorate it in a soothing fashion different from the way the rest of the organization is decorated (pastel colors, floor pillows, relaxing art such as seascapes).

During Conflict

Call for a time out when conflict, tension, or emotions are interfering with:
- Decision making.

- Ability to lead.

- Group dynamics.

- Problem-solving.

A time out can be as useful for others as it is for you. Others' emotional distress, hurt feelings, or need for a break may be indicated by:
- Facial expressions.

- Difficulty staying in control.

- Avoiding eye contact.

- Tone of voice.

- Appearing distracted or bored.

Remind yourself that a time out:
- Does not mean avoiding or ignoring the conflict.

- Lets you choose the right response by delaying your first response.

During time out, as you use the deep breathing technique, replace stressful thoughts with reassuring ones.
- I'm upset right now, but this is a good organization with good people.

- This isn't personal. It's not about me.

- I control my emotions; they don't control me.

After calming down, re-focus and make good use of your time out.
- Engage in reflective thinking.

- Take the perspective of others.

- Develop a thorough understanding of the situation by gathering additional information or talking to others.

- Devise a plan for conflict resolution.

After returning from time out:
- Apologize if necessary.

- Express appreciation for others' patience and understanding.

- Return to confronting the conflict constructively.

After Conflict

Assess yourself.
- What did I do well?

- What areas still need improvement?

- Did I make good use of my time out?

- How will others view me and my actions?

- If the conflict remains, is it due to my not delaying my immediate reaction?

_____

_____

_____

_____

_____

_____

_____

_____

_____

_____

_____

Seek feedback from trusted others.

- Did I return from time out calmer and more focused?

- Was I attentive to others' need for a time out?

_____

_____

_____

_____

_____

_____

_____

_____

_____

_____

_____

_____

Follow up with the person with whom you were in conflict.

- If the conflict seems to be at an impasse, try a longer time out, even several days if possible.

Motto:
Time out,
not cop out.

CONTROLLING ANGER

We boil at different degrees.
Benjamin Franklin

Dynamic Example:

Dean's temper was legendary. Nearly everyone in the company had a favorite "Guillotine Dean" story; the obscenity-filled tantrum when the budget was cut was especially well-known. Although the explosive mood swings and short fuse led to a high turnover rate in his department, Dean's outbursts were tolerated by upper management because they "show he's passionate about his work." As long as his frightened and intimidated workers produced on time and under budget, Dean's job was safe and his abusive rants permitted.

A particularly harmful response to conflict is a display of anger toward the other person by raising one's voice, using harsh words, and so forth. Such displays frequently lead to an escalation of the conflict, and make it more likely that the conflict will focus on personalities rather issues. Angry outbursts frighten and intimidate not only the target but also others who are within earshot or who become aware of one's reputation as a "hot-head."

Intimidation is, in fact, one of the main functions of anger. By creating a situation in which others are too frightened to question one's authority and decisions, a broad base of power can be established. Unfortunately, this is often dysfunctional not only for interpersonal relationships, but also for the organization. Displays of anger inhibit and destroy the trust, teamwork, and open communication that are required for good decision making and positive work relationships.

Sometimes anger is expressed in order to ensure that mistakes don't happen again. This attempt to "teach a lesson" may occasionally work, but it is usually at the expense of good interpersonal relationships. Just as frequently, however, displays of anger *don't* succeed, and the quality of work does not improve. In fact, angry outbursts may diminish the quality of work and even lead to calculated sabotage. The hostility, fear, and intimidation engendered by displays of anger are simply not conducive to "teaching."

In addition to the target and the organization, anger can be detrimental to those who get angry. Tantrums and hostile outbursts hinder promotions and raises because they indicate that one lacks the impulse control and people skills necessary to manage, motivate, and lead. This is true even in professions where some aggressiveness might be rewarded. Anger is also harmful in physical ways. Decades of scientific research have linked anger with hypertension, migraines, ulcers, depression, coronary problems, and immune system disorders. In short, anger hurts not only others, it hurts you.

Anger, like other emotions, is controllable. For instance, while you might often be angry at your boss, you seldom, if ever, yell at him or her, because you fear the consequences enough either to swallow your anger or express it in a suitable manner. If you can control your anger in some situations *and you can*, you can control it in all. Feeling angry is okay but expressing anger in a hostile and aggressive manner is not. Your goal is to control the anger you feel and express it in a more acceptable manner.

Before Conflict

Begin with Reflection Questions.
- Which situations or people provoke my anger?

- What behaviors or statements by others trigger my anger?

- In what situations have I felt angry but controlled it? Why?

- What have been the personal and professional consequences of my displays of anger?

- How do I interact with people with whom I've had disagreements?

- How do I want to be viewed when the conflict is over?

_____

_____

_____

_____

_____

_____

_____

_____

_____

_____

_____

Practice expressing your anger in a more acceptable manner (see Expressing Emotions, Page 51).
- I am angry because . . . .

- I am disappointed at what has occurred.

- Although I am angry, I want to discuss this calmly.

- I'm angry right now and want a time-out before proceeding.

Study Taking Time Outs (Page 39), especially:
- The deep breathing technique.

- The methods of time out you will take in particular types of situations.

Remind yourself that emotions are learned responses and can be controlled through thoughts and behavior.
- I control my anger. It doesn't control me.

- If I lose it, I lose.

- I will eliminate thoughts of retaliation and retribution.

During Conflict

Count down before you blast off.
- Slow your anger with controlled deep breathing.

- Delay responding until you are calm.

- Remind yourself: "I am in control and the anger I feel will pass."

- Reframe "You make me angry" to "I will deal with my anger constructively."

If you feel yourself about to erupt, STOP!
- Remind yourself that "Angry" is not the image you want to present. Your goal is control.

- Mentally schedule a private appointment with yourself during which time you will rant, rave, scream, or otherwise express how you're feeling.

- Keep your appointment with yourself. Let it all out; you'll feel better.

Explain clearly and calmly that you are angry and why.

- *Don't yell.* Increasing your volume will only escalate conflict and tension.

- Don't shoot the messenger. Be sure your anger is focused in the right direction.

- Avoid hasty judgements about the value and worth of the person.

Criticizing Constructively (Page 34) is an important element of expressing anger in an appropriate way, especially these points:

- Emphasize that your goal is not personal but professional — to improve the organization's functioning and environment.

- Begin sentences with "I" rather than "You."

- Express your anger as "disappointment" at the person's actions and the consequences of those actions for the organization, rather than directing anger at the person's personality or intellect.

- Balance any expressed anger with appreciation for work well done.

If it's necessary to soothe hurt feelings, try Reaching Out (Page 47), especially these points:

- Look for signs of emotional distress.

- Provide time for the other person to compose him/herself.

- If appropriate, admit your responsibility, apologize, and ask what you can do to make amends.

After Conflict

Assess yourself.
- What did I do well?

- What areas still need improvement?

- Did I express understanding?

- Did I listen patiently?

- Was I aware of my body language, facial expressions, and tone of voice?

- How will others view me and my actions?

- If the conflict remains, is it because I did not control my anger?

_____

_____

_____

_____

_____

_____

_____

_____

_____

_____

Seek feedback from trusted others.
- Did I express my anger appropriately?

- Were my nonverbal cues such as voice and facial expression calm and not angry?

- Did I understand the other person's point of view?

_____

_____

_____

_____

_____

_____

_____

Follow up with the person with whom you were in conflict.

- Cool down, then personally apologize to all concerned.

- Take responsibility for your statements and tone. *Don't* put the blame elsewhere.

- Discuss the conflict and your anger tactfully, sensitively and privately.

- Ensure that the relationship is back on track.

- Express appreciation for work well done.

Cope with the strain of pent-up anger through:

- Relaxation techniques such as massage or deep breathing.

- Meditation or yoga.

- Vigorous physical exercise.

- Involvement in outside hobbies or interests.

- Venting to trusted others.

If you have tried all (or at least most) of these techniques and are still unable to get your anger under control, it may be necessary to take an anger management class or seek counseling from a competent professional. This is particularly recommended if your anger continues to be:

- Detrimental to your work.

- Interfering with personal relationships.

- Harmful to your health and well-being.

- Holding you back from being the person you want to be.

- Out of your control.

Motto:
If I lose it, I lose.

REACHING OUT

No act of kindness, no matter how small, is ever wasted.

Aesop

Dynamic Example:

Michael expected that re-organizing his department's personnel, duties, and office space would cause some consternation and conflict. After all, he reasoned, there are some complainers in every group. But believing that the benefits would outweigh the costs, he announced his plans at the weekly meeting. He was taken by surprise, however, at the range and degree of emotions his staff expressed: frustration, tears, hurt, disappointment, anger, stony silence. Unprepared for such strong emotional upheaval, Michael paused momentarily, then proceeded as if everyone was in agreement with his plans. He ended by declaring that the re-organization would become effective the next day.

By reaching out to the other person, one can often repair any emotional damage caused by a conflict. This may involve calming the other person down, soothing hurt feelings, or making amends. The goal of this strategy is to reduce the emotional tension in the situation and allow resumption of the conflict resolution process. While one may feel that repairing emotions is time-consuming, unnecessary or inappropriately personal in the workplace, consider the consequences of not doing so: protracted conflict, a reputation as an insensitive bully, unhappy distressed workers performing poorly, sabotage, and unfortunately all too commonly today, workplace violence.

Reaching out early and often may prevent serious problems from developing.

Coping with emotional distress (yours as well as others) can, admittedly, be difficult and stress-inducing. You may be faced with tears, yelling, and looks of hatred all in the space of a few seconds. The emotions may be directed at superiors, subordinates, the organization, the situation, the world, or, most difficult of all, you. It could all be as overwhelming for you as it is for the person you're trying to help. But if you can remain calm, attentive and alert, you will be able to discern what the other person needs: sympathy, comfort, commiseration, or just someone to listen. Because everyone differs in his/her level of sensitivity and comfort with physical contact, it is not advisable to pat, hug, or otherwise touch a distressed co-worker. Listening will often be the first, best, and sometimes only thing you can do.

Before Conflict

Begin with Reflection Questions.
- When in past conflicts would taking time to reach out have been beneficial?

- What have been the personal and professional consequences of not reaching out?

- What kinds of reaching out am I most comfortable with? Least comfortable?

- How do I want to be viewed when the conflict is over?

_____

_____

_____

_____

_____

_____

_____

_____

_____

_____

_____

_____

_____

_____

Anticipate what could happen during a conflict.

- What emotions might arise and why?

- How would I handle different emotional scenarios?

- Would the presence of a third party be helpful?

- Can the meeting time be arranged to occur near the end of the day or week so as to allow a natural cooling-off period?

_____

_____

_____

_____

_____

_____

_____

_____

_____

_____

_____

Break down barriers and build bridges.

- Pay attention to others. Be thoughtful, empathetic, and supportive.

- If aware of personal difficulties someone is having, express your concern with a card, visit, or phone call.

- Take (or make) the opportunity to talk informally with others, take them to lunch, acknowledge their birthdays, etc.

_____

_____

_____

_____

_____

_____

_____

_____

_____

During Conflict

Try to identify the person's emotional state so that you can respond most effectively.

- Anger

- Fear

- Anxiety

- Guilt

- Remorse

Cues as to one's emotional state will be signaled by:

- Facial expressions.

- Difficulty staying in control.

- Avoiding eye contact.

- Tone of voice.

- Body posture.

Directly acknowledge others' emotions and their emotional needs.
- *Never* say one is wrong to feel the way s/he is feeling.

- Encourage the other person to express his/her feelings.

- Express your sincere desire to understand.

- Be accepting and respectful.

Employ Dynamic Listening (Page 25), especially these points:
- Take the other person's perspective.

- Be sure you understand the other's position and feelings. Ask questions.

- Empathize; let the other person know when you understand and when you don't.

Provide time for the other person to compose him/herself.
- Request a time out.

- Change the subject.

- Postpone the discussion until another time.

If you are the cause of another's emotional distress:
- Admit your responsibility.

- Sincerely apologize.

- If appropriate, ask what you can do to make amends.

- Praise or otherwise "give strokes" to improve the emotional climate.

After Conflict

Assess yourself.
- What did I do well?

- What areas still need improvement?

- Did I correctly anticipate which emotions would develop?

- How will others view me and my actions?

- If the conflict remains, is it because I have not addressed others' emotional needs?

_____

_____

_____

_____

_____

_____

_____

_____

_____

_____

_____

Seek feedback from trusted others.
- Was I sensitive to the other person's needs?

- Did I accurately read the other's verbal and nonverbal cues to his/her emotional state?

- Was I effective in my attempts to reach out?

_____

_____

_____

_____

_____

_____

_____

_____

Follow up with the person with whom you were in conflict.

- Check on the emotional status of the other person. Be supportive but not intrusive.

- Apologize if you did not do so earlier. It's never too late.

- If the other person is still distressed, it might be appropriate to suggest s/he talk to a third party, such as human resources personnel or a counselor.

If you are concerned that the other person is so distraught as to be dangerous to him/herself or others:

- Don't threaten, criticize, or intimidate.

- Establish trust but don't make any commitments you can't keep.

- Attempt to resolve the most critical issues first.

- Express your concerns to the appropriate person or department in your organization.

- Review the organization's safety and security plans for protecting its employees, or help develop such plans if they do not already exist.

Motto:
Break down barriers;
build bridges.

EXPRESSING EMOTIONS

Never apologize for showing feeling. When you do so, you apologize for the truth.
Benjamin Disraeli

Dynamic Example:

On the spur of the moment, Ellen called a meeting of the advertising department. Although Marty's assistant was included, Marty was not because Ellen felt this involved issues so minor they could be handled by his assistant and not take up his valuable time. Marty, however, felt hurt and embarrassed at being overlooked in such an obvious way. After thinking about it for a few days, he became concerned: Was there a hidden message in Ellen's action? Soon his hurt and anxiety turned to anger. He worked hard, deserved better, and vowed to get even. When Marty solicited donations for a retirement gift for an outgoing vice-president, he didn't approach Ellen. Hers was the only name missing from the ad department's card. Ellen's hurt and embarrassment were matched by her confusion; obviously Marty's "oversight" was intentional, but she had no idea why. However, she decided, if he could play childish games, well then, so could she.

One potentially destructive way an individual can respond to conflict is by not expressing his or her emotional reaction to the conflict. Instead the person conceals these emotions from others and keeps them inside. While there is some value in not expressing all of one's emotional responses during a conflict, hiding relevant feelings can be stumbling blocks on the path to conflict resolution. Hidden emotions can also negatively affect job performance, relationships with co-workers, and loyalty to the organization. In addition, unexpressed emotions can cause depression, insomnia, headaches and other emotional and physical ailments.

There are two forms that hidden emotions can take. One, *unexpressed emotions*, involves keeping feelings bottled up inside where they are primarily a source of stress and discomfort to the person feeling them. The second, *inappropriately expressed emotions*, involves directing one's feelings against the person with whom one is in conflict. Rather than openly discussing one's hurt, envy, or most commonly anger, the individual tries to get even by giving the other person a "taste of his own medicine." Such retaliation tends in many cases to further escalate the conflict, because what one person sees as action that evens things out, others interpret as fresh provocation. The result is that problems persist and conflicts perpetuate. Rather than openly discussing feelings and resolving what begins as a minor problem, conflict persists and escalates. Hurt and anger continue to build, and good relationships may be destroyed.

There are a variety of reasons why one might keep one's feelings inside — belief that they can't be expressed properly, fear of making the situation worse, or fear of losing acceptance or validation from others. Perhaps of greatest concern is that expressing one's emotions is inappropriate for a business situation. However, when unexpressed emotions are interfering with conflict resolution or productive relationships with co-workers, then it is necessary to address them so as to get on with business.

Providing information to others about how you feel and why can be useful to them; it tells them the issue is important to you and something which should not be overlooked during conflict resolution. It also indicates that you care about your relationships with others. The goal here is to express your emotions in a manner appropriate for a business situation. You don't want to come across as a whiner or complainer. Nor do you want the person with whom you are in conflict to feel at fault for your feelings. Instead, you want to consider which of your feelings are relevant to the conflict resolution process and express them in a manner that is honest, thoughtful, and controlled.

Before Conflict

Begin with Reflection Questions.
- In past conflicts, have my hidden emotions undermined the conflict resolution process?

- Are certain emotions more difficult for me to express? Why?

- Do I tend to blame others for feeling as I do?

- How can I describe my feelings in words that are informative yet cast no blame?

- What have been the personal and professional consequences of hiding my emotions?

- How do I want to be viewed when the conflict is over?

_____

_____

_____

_____

_____

Practice expressing information about your emotional state in ways that cast no blame.
- I feel uncomfortable with that solution.

- I am angry right now and I need a time-out.

- I feel this way because . . . .

If you tend to respond to conflict by retaliating:
- Consider the costs of retaliation for you, others, and the organization.

- Depersonalize the conflict. View it as a conflict of ideas or approaches, rather than of people.

- Reframe "I'll get even" to "I will turn my anger into motivation."

During Conflict

Remind yourself:
- How I feel is important to the conflict resolution process.

- I can express my emotions in a professional manner.

- I will not be defensive or cast blame.

Before speaking, be sure the emotions are worth expressing.

- Will expressing my emotions be beneficial to the conflict resolution process?

- Am I providing the other person with useful information about how I feel and why?

- Once expressed, is there something that the other person can do about how I feel?

Explain how you feel and why.

- Request a time out if you need to think about how you want to express yourself.

- Choose your words carefully. Keep them courteous and professional.

- Describe your emotional state. Be calm, not out-of-control.

- Be specific: "I feel bad" is not informative. Instead say: "I am frustrated (or angry or disappointed, etc.) because . . . ."

- Solicit information concerning how well the other person understands your feelings.

Don't blame the other person for how you feel. Use "I" instead of "You."

- "I am hurt by this situation," rather than "You hurt my feelings."

- "I am angry," instead of "You make me so mad!"

- "I am disappointed that the conflict has come to this point," not "You are to blame for this mess."

- Clarify a statement that is hurtful or seems meant as insult. "I don't think you meant this but it sounds as if what you said was. . . ."

If you feel you're about to cry, get angry, or otherwise inappropriately express your emotions, STOP!

- Remind yourself that crying, tantrums, etc. will not present the image you want to project.

- Mentally schedule a private appointment with yourself during which time you will cry, scream, or otherwise express how you're feeling.

- Keep your appointment with yourself. Let it all out; you'll feel better.

If you tend to retaliate when faced with a conflict, respond positively instead.

- Be the bigger person. Make the first move to stop the conflict cycle.

- Turn the other cheek. Respect, and if necessary, forgive the other person.

- Build a rewarding and positive relationship.

- Calmly and without casting blame, explain why you feel angry, frustrated, or hurt.

After Conflict

Assess yourself.

- What did I do well?

- What areas still need improvement?

- Did my body language or nonverbal cues express my unspoken emotions?

- How will others view me and my actions?

- If the conflict remains, is it because my emotions remain hidden and are interfering with the resolution process?

_____

_____

_____

_____

_____

Seek feedback from trusted others.
- Was I honest and informative when expressing my feelings?

- Did I avoid expressing my emotions, especially when doing so would have been helpful?

- Did I solicit others' level of understanding of what I was trying to express?

_____

_____

_____

_____

_____

_____

_____

_____

_____

_____

Follow up with the person with whom you were in conflict.
- If necessary, try again to express your emotions.

- Check with the person for his/her level of understanding.

- Encourage the other person to express his/her feelings.

Cope with the strain of unexpressed emotions through:
- Relaxation techniques (massage your neck, breathe deeply, look out the window, etc.).

- Meditation or yoga.

- Vigorous physical exercise.

- Involvement in outside hobbies or interests.

- Confiding in a supportive co-worker or friend.

Problems affect people differently. What may not be a problem for some may be a serious one for others. Take an assertiveness training course or seek counseling from a competent professional if your hidden emotions seem to be:
- Detrimental to your work.

- Interfering with personal relationships.

- Harmful to your health and well-being.

- Holding you back from being the person you want to be.

Motto:
Express it –
don't suppress it.

Resolving Conflict

The previous two sections addressed Building Relationships and Managing Emotions as ways to deal constructively with conflict. These sections set the stage and make possible the use of specific problem-solving techniques that are necessary for resolving conflicts successfully. When relationships are in tatters or emotions have run riot, it may well be impossible to effectively utilize these methods. Once the stage is set, however, the use of these techniques holds the greatest chance of resolving conflicts to the satisfaction of all concerned.

This section then builds upon the preceding ones by describing step-by-step how to resolve workplace conflicts. ***Taking Action*** urges patience, persistence, and a commitment to moving forward. Flexibility and reciprocity are the keys to ***Cooperating***. ***Dynamic Conflict Resolution*** incorporates all the methods of responding to conflict described up to this point in the guide, but goes beyond as well to specific tactics and strategies that are not included elsewhere. Through a process of listening, communicating, brainstorming and negotiating, Dynamic Conflict Resolution can result in solutions that meet everyone's needs. Although this process requires time, energy, patience and commitment, you will find that the benefits of Dynamic Conflict Resolution for everyone involved and the organization as a whole are well worth the effort.

Top Tips For Resolving Conflict

1. Attack problems, not people.

2. Build consensus, not conflict.

3. Communicate.

4. Cooperate.

5. Collaborate.

TAKING ACTION

Don't wait for your ship to come in — swim out to it.
Anonymous

Dynamic Example:

Caroline had presented her supervisor Jim with an innovative proposal aimed at saving their department a substantial sum of money. Each week when she inquired about its status, Jim would reply "It's in the pipeline," leading Caroline to believe that he had acted upon it and that it was on its way up the chain of command. In fact the proposal was on his desk, still unexamined after several weeks. Since Caroline knew of Jim's tendency to procrastinate, she became increasingly frustrated and suspicious as time passed. As her questions became more pointed and her tone more irritated, Jim began to avoid her. He would take a circuitous route to the coffee room so as to avoid walking past her cubicle and brought lunch from home to eat in his office so they would not run into each other in the cafeteria. After two months of waiting, Caroline went over Jim's head to the department supervisor. While this resulted in her proposal being enacted, it also caused hurt, anger, and continued conflict.

One of the most common ways to deal with conflict is by not dealing with it at all. Rather than directly confronting the problem, a passive and ineffectual method is taken. Avoiding the issue or the person, or simply giving in and giving up are examples of inaction. Because the conflict is ignored, these strategies tend to perpetuate, rather than resolve, conflict. One particularly negative consequence of inaction is that it reflects badly on the person. The individual who gives in, postpones, avoids, or obstructs earns a reputation as someone who is neither a team-player nor a leader. Organizations view passivity or inactivity as indicative of a lack of motivation, trustworthiness, reliability, and initiative.

The constructive way to respond to conflict is by remaining involved and taking action. This requires maintaining contact with the other person and trying to move forward or make a fresh start. While one might feel tempted to hide out and do nothing, it is imperative to remain involved and actively take steps to find a workable solution that satisfies both parties. This can only be accomplished by bringing the conflict into the open and confronting it constructively.

The first step to taking action requires a bit of self-analysis: What form does my inaction take, and why do I avoid taking action? Individuals who avoid action by stonewalling or obstructing others may do so out of anger, a need to retaliate, or a desire to control others. Those who ignore or avoid their adversary or simply give in may be acting out of fear — fear of conflict, fear of reprisals if confrontation occurs, fear of making the situation worse, fear of losing control of one's emotions in front of others, fear of disapproval or of not being accepted. Often accompanying fear is an element of wishful thinking, as in "I wish this problem would go away," or "I hope this problem fixes itself." Because this will rarely happen, it is necessary to brace yourself and actively and directly confront the conflict.

Before Conflict

Begin with Reflection Questions.
- What form(s) does my inaction take?
- Why do I avoid taking action?
- What have been the personal and professional consequences of my inaction?
- What are the advantages of taking action for me, others, and the organization?
- How do I want to be viewed when the conflict is over?

_____

_____

_____

_____

_____

_____

_____

_____

_____

_____

_____

Think thoughts that get you moving forward.
- A forceful style is sometimes necessary.
- I don't have to like someone in order to work with him/her.
- Taking the initiative to make a fresh start will reflect well on me.
- I expect to do well.
- Feel the fear and do it anyway.

View obstacles as challenges.
- Envision what you want; remember why taking action is necessary.

- Focus on the things you have control over and can change. Push yourself to create solutions.

- Enlist others to look at the conflict objectively and help search for solutions.

- Anticipate what others will question or resist, and prepare your response.
- Set goals and deadlines for action. Act on your plans on the appointed dates.

- Make a public commitment to take action. Then take it.

During Conflict

Small steps count.
- Start by making contact with the other person in a manner that will be most comfortable to him/her (voice-mail message, a note, water-cooler chatting with others around).

- Make amends if necessary, first privately, then publicly.

- Continue your progress by tackling more easily-resolved issues first, then working up to more complicated ones.

Build a good relationship.
- Be respectful, courteous, and open-minded.

- Ask what you can do to improve the relationship. _Listen_ to the answer.

- Express diplomatically what the other person can do as well.

- As needed, take the other's perspective (see Dynamic Listening, Page 25).

- When necessary, repair emotions (see Reaching Out, Page 47).

Confront the conflict constructively (see Dynamic Conflict Resolution, Page 64).
- Communicate frankly and openly with the other person.

- Show your sincere desire to resolve the conflict.

- Address the problem. Be direct but not aggressive.

- Work *with* the other person to resolve it.

If you meet with resistance, don't concede immediately. Remind yourself that you will need to be persistent.
- Replace "I can't do this," with "This may be difficult, but I will try to do it."

- If I can't agree to a proposal, I will say no clearly and explain my position.

- When I don't understand, I will get clarification.

- During negotiations, I will not be swayed by extreme offers.

- Should others want me to give in or should the situation become difficult, I will stand my ground and show my integrity.

If you tend to stonewall or obstruct others when faced with a conflict:
- Reframe "I won't" and "It can't be done," to "I believe we can," or "Let's explore that suggestion."

- Share information in a timely fashion and in sufficient detail so as to allow tasks to be accomplished.

- Depersonalize the conflict. It's not about people, it's about issues.

- Accept others for who they are. Treat others the way they want to be treated.

- Vow "I will channel my anger in constructive and productive ways."

Keep your eyes on the prize.
- Focus on the value of taking action and moving forward.

- Remember that a productive, continuing relationship will benefit all concerned.

- Anticipate how good it will feel when the conflict is resolved and your goal is accomplished.

After Conflict

Assess yourself.
- What did I do well?

- What areas still need improvement?

- Did I make steady, measurable progress?

- How will others view me and my actions?

- If the conflict remains, is it due to a lack of effort on my part?

_____

_____

_____

_____

_____

_____

_____

_____

Seek feedback from trusted others.
- Were my efforts at moving forward direct and constructive?

- Did I communicate my position and concerns openly and clearly?

- Was I sensitive to the other party in my actions?

_____   _____
_____   _____
_____   _____
_____   _____
_____   _____
_____   _____
_____   _____
_____   _____
_____   _____
_____

Follow up with the person with whom you   _____
were in conflict.

   • Continue to take action and make steady   _____
     progress forward. Remember even small
     steps count.   _____

   • Establish that your relationship remains   _____
     professional and on good terms.
          _____

If the conflict remains unresolved: _____

   • First, allow some time to pass. Let
     emotions cool down.   _____

   • Enlist others to look at the conflict   _____
     objectively and help search for solutions.
          _____
   • Try again to resolve the conflict, either
     face-to-face or in writing.   _____

          _____

          _____

Motto:
Feel the fear and   _____
do it anyway.
          _____

          _____

COOPERATING

One of the first principles of perseverance is to know when to stop persevering.

Carolyn Wells

Dynamic Example:

Janet had been trampled by Luke in the past but that had been over big issues. Today Janet simply needed use of the conference room Luke had already scheduled and thought this would be easy to resolve. First, she asked to trade her smaller room as Luke's group of five needed less space than her group of twenty — Luke said "No." Next, she suggested a room with a better view — "No." Then she requested use of the room for a half-day rather than the full day she actually needed — "No." Finally, Janet tried humor and friendliness — "No." Angered by the encounter, Janet gave up, but she silently resolved never to cooperate with Luke when he needed something.

While holding to a position can at times be an effective negotiating strategy, an absolute refusal to consider changing your stance during a conflict is a destructive behavior. When the goal in a negotiation is to crush the opposition by gaining concessions, it can have long-lasting, detrimental effects. A "winning is everything" strategy causes hurt, embarrassment, anger, and a loss of goodwill. With the designation of one party as a "loser" comes feelings and perceptions of failure, inequality, powerlessness, and anger. Thus while a competitive, must-win strategy may be effective in some areas, it is detrimental for interpersonal relationships or situations which require trust or teamwork.

A second negative outcome of the must-win strategy is that it often creates extreme positions for both parties. The harder you push, the more others will resist. The more others resist, the more you dig in Psychologists call this process *reactance* and cite the classic example of parents who dislike their daughter's delinquent boyfriend. The more the parents complain and try to keep the two apart, the more she wants to be with him. The more she defies her parents, the angrier and more punitive they become. What had been a loving, trusting parent-child relationship has become a war.

An alternative strategy is cooperation, an approach where the goal is not win/lose, but rather win/win. The "everyone wins" method of conflict resolution requires replacing competitiveness with flexibility, reciprocity, and an attitude of "all for one." The goal is to resolve the conflict in a way that, as much as is possible, satisfies everyone.

Before Conflict

Begin with Reflection Questions.
- Do I value competition over cooperation?

- Am I resistant to being influenced?

- What have been the personal and professional consequences of a "winning at all costs" strategy?

- If I "win," will the "losers" cooperate with me in the future?

- How do I want to be viewed when the conflict is over?

_____

_____

_____

_____

_____

_____

_____

_____

_____

_____

_____

_____

_____

_____

Prepare your position.
- What is your fundamental goal? That is, what is it you *really* want or need?

- What is the maximum you desire?

- What is the minimum you will accept?

- What alternatives would be acceptable?

_____

_____

_____

_____

_____

_____

_____

_____

_____

_____

_____

_____

_____

Organize the issues into categories based upon your willingness to compromise.
- Disposable: wants or desires to be used as conciliatory gestures.

- Non-essential: would be nice to have but not critical.

- Essential: needs and "must have" issues.

_____

_____

_____

_____

_____

_____

_____

_____

_____

_____

_____

_____

Tell yourself:
- I will be cooperative rather than competitive.

- I will be flexible, reasonable and open-minded.

- Reciprocity requires reasonable concessions.

- *We* can make it a win one for everyone.

Gain the support of influential others.
- Meet with them beforehand.

- Explain your position.

- Express your desire to make it a win/win situation.

During Conflict

Take a reasonable stand. Don't "lock in" your position.

- State your position clearly and calmly once or twice.

- Give others time to digest new and unfamiliar ideas and facts.

- Express your flexibility and open-mindedness.

- Avoid hard bargaining and phrases like "take it or leave it."

- *Never* resort to threats.

Remind yourself:

- What I *want* and what I *need* are two different things.

- I will compromise in order to be viewed as a cooperative person.

- It's not "me against you" but "us against the problem."

- Our goal is not to win and lose, but to win and win.

Be looking for an acceptable compromise. Ask the other party:

- What is the minimum you will accept?

- What would you prefer?

- Are my assumptions correct?

- What is the best outcome for both parties?

Dynamic Communication (Page 29) is critical here, especially these points:

- Restate your understanding of the concerns and problems raised.

- Make your points in a non-threatening way by asking questions.

- Preface your opinions with "I think" or "One possible approach is . . . ."

- Recognize when others are resisting your agenda.

Dynamic Conflict Resolution (Page 64) is important here, especially these points:

- Balance your position with an acknowledgement of common ground.

- Agree to disagree. Establish where disagreements can co-exist.

- Brainstorm to create solutions that are advantageous to everyone concerned.

- Select solutions that best meet all parties' needs.

If resolution appears unlikely at this time:

- Emphasize your willingness to work together to find a mutually satisfactory solution.

- Suggest further discussion at another time.

- Follow up with specific solutions.

After Conflict

Assess yourself.

- What did I do well?

- What areas still need improvement?

- Were needs met — mine as well as others'?

- How will others view me and my actions?

- If the conflict remains, is it due to my unwillingness to compromise or my lack of cooperation?

_____

_____

_____

_____

_____

_____

_____

_____

_____

_____

_____

_____

_____

If the conflict remains unresolved:
- Evaluate why, particularly your role in the impasse. Have you done all you can to be cooperative?

- State your continued willingness to work together to resolve the conflict.

- Invite a neutral third party to help resolve the conflict.

Seek feedback from trusted others.
- Was I sensitive to the other party's needs and wants?

- Was I reasonable in my needs and wants?

- Did I employ hard bargaining tactics or phrases?

> *Motto:*
> *Win one for everyone.*

_____

_____

_____

_____

_____

_____

_____

Follow up with the person with whom you were in conflict.
- Ask: "Did I go too far or not far enough?"

- Ensure that your relationship remains friendly and professional.

_____

_____

_____

_____

_____

_____

_____

_____

_____

_____

_____

_____

_____

_____

_____

_____

_____

_____

_____

DYNAMIC CONFLICT RESOLUTION

There never was a good war or a bad peace.

Benjamin Franklin

Dynamic Example:

Amy and Brett had been at loggerheads over the budget for several weeks. At each meeting to attempt resolution, things began calmly enough but eventually tensions began to rise and their pledges to cooperate vanished. Rather than trying to understand each other's point of view or create possible solutions, they sat in frustrated silence, each expecting the other to give in. Amy's attempt to move things along consisted of asking Brett on which items he was willing to compromise. Since it was clear that compromise applied only to him, Brett answered "Nothing." Neither gave any thought to how their prolonged impasse was affecting the morale of their respective departments, nor that they appeared to their superiors to be stubborn, argumentative, and ill-suited to leadership positions.

Dynamic Conflict Resolution is a collaborative means of resolving disputes. This non-adversarial method of problem-solving is rooted in each party's commitment to achieving a mutually satisfactory solution. Through a process of listening, communicating, brainstorming and negotiating, Dynamic Conflict Resolution not only increases understanding, but also eases the resolution of future problems. It is especially useful when there is a need to establish and maintain long-term, trusting, cooperative relationships. The goal of Dynamic Conflict Resolution is to work out disputes and disagreements in a manner that provides a fair return for all involved while maintaining harmonious relationships.

Dynamic Conflict Resolution can be a challenging process. It requires effort, energy, and patience as well as negotiating, listening, communicating, cooperation, emotional management and other skills described throughout **Managing Conflict Dynamics**. Yet even in an organization or field where competition and aggressiveness are prized, the ability to resolve conflicts (your own as well as others') can be invaluable and will only reflect well on you. Considering the long-term costs of recurring problems and hostile relationships, a collaborative approach that is constructive and fair is a process that can produce solutions for everyone involved.

The key to conflict resolution is creating solutions to the problem. This could involve brainstorming to generate new ideas, devising creative responses to the conflict, or engaging others in the search for solutions. Although creating and agreeing on solutions requires time, energy and the cooperation of the other party, the benefits of conflict resolution for all involved and the organization as a whole are worth the efforts.

Before starting the conflict resolution process, however, it is necessary to establish the root of the conflict. That is, what are the underlying (usually unmentioned) issues at the center of the storm? One's need for power, control, self-esteem, or revenge are often the *real* issues. One of the first steps then to conflict resolution is understanding what motivates one's self as well as others and uncovering alternative ways to meet needs.

Before Conflict

Begin with Reflection Questions.
- What is at the root of this conflict?

- Does this conflict signal issues I have neglected or problems I have overlooked?
- What have been the personal and professional consequences of not resolving conflicts?

- In which conflicts in the past would brainstorming have been beneficial? How?

- How do I want to be viewed when the conflict is over?

_____

_____

_____

_____

_____

_____

_____

_____

_____

_____

_____

_____

Think thoughts that move you towards conflict resolution.
- This conflict is an opportunity to strengthen our relationship.

- The process requires courtesy, patience, self-control, tact, reasonableness, and forgiveness.

- I will put my assumptions aside.

- I won't reject others' positions out of hand.

Do your homework.
- Learn as much as possible about the other person and his/her position.

- Research and develop multiple solutions to the problem. Have them ready to present at an opportune time.
- Read books and articles about successful negotiators and how they work.

Plan *what* you are going to say and *why* you are saying it.
- Identify your needs and interests.

- Identify practical limitations.

- Anticipate the other parties' demands, positions, version of the facts, needs, strengths, and weaknesses.

- Develop solutions that meet *others'* needs as well as your own.

Plan *how* you are going to say it.
- Choose your words carefully. Keep them friendly, respectful, and courteous.

- Practice your speech with a friend or co-worker.

- Listen to yourself from the other's point of view. How would you feel if someone said those things to you?

Pick your moment.
- Wait for an appropriate time when emotions are calm and the other person has the time in which to focus on the problem.

- Select a neutral, non-threatening place in which to meet.

- Provide snacks and decaffeinated beverages.

During Conflict

Establish an atmosphere that encourages openness, constructive criticism, and problem-solving.
- Ascertain that everyone involved is present, focused on the problem, and committed to finding solutions.
- Specify the consequences of not resolving the conflict.

Lay out the ground rules.
- Be respectful.

- Keep an open mind.

- Don't interrupt.

- Don't display anger.

- Don't use profanity, violence or other actions that may be interpreted as aggression.

Examine the conflict from all points of view.
- Encourage everyone involved to describe the conflict from his/her own perspective.

- Identify each other's motives, goals, and agendas.

- Discuss only those past issues that are relevant to the current conflict.

- Do not permit "blamestorming," that is, group discussion and assignment of blame for the conflict.

Ensure that you understand the other person's point of view (see Dynamic Listening, Page 25).
- Restate or paraphrase what you think is being said.

- Ask for examples to clarify the issues.

- Take responsibility for not understanding.

- Acknowledge the other's position without agreeing with it by saying "That's an interesting point of view," or "Many people have that same position."

Next, accentuate the positive.
- Identify points of mutual agreement and mutual dependence.

- Emphasize that you want to work *together* towards a mutually satisfactory solution.

Next, confront the conflicts constructively.
- Handle the disagreements one at a time to maintain focus and control emotions.

- Begin with an issue that will be easy to resolve and work up to more difficult ones.

- State facts and information first.

- State your needs, then listen until you understand the needs of the other person.

- Express an alternative point of view in the form of a question, such as "Would another solution be X?"

Brainstorm every possible solution.
- List every idea no matter how unrealistic. Don't evaluate them, just list them.

- Expand on each other's ideas.

- Have some fun! Developing and exploring silly solutions will create laughter, reduce tension, and contribute to a positive atmosphere.

Next, begin evaluating the alternatives.
- List the pros and cons of each.

- Remain focused on the desired outcome.

- Gradually narrow down the choices to the best two or three.

- Avoid "winners" and "losers." Select the outcome which most effectively serves the organization.

- Be willing to compromise. Remember: you're looking for a solution, not a victory.

- Establish what needs to be done in order to implement the solution (who will do what, when, where, and how).

- Share the decision-making.

If you face resistance on the grounds that Dynamic Conflict Resolution is too time-consuming, inefficient, or disruptive:
- Outline the long-term costs of recurring problems and hostile relationships.

- Emphasize that a collaborative approach is a fair, constructive process aimed at producing solutions for everyone involved.

Throughout the process, monitor and directly address your and others':
- Emotional states, particularly anger and distress.

- Tendency to get off track or digress.

- Substitution of opinion and generalities for facts and analysis.

- Temptation to engage in a win/lose style.

Focus on the future.
- Speak in the future tense rather than past tense.

- Emphasize your and others' intentions and goals rather than past behaviors and problems.

- Highlight opportunities for future accomplishments rather than past shortcomings and failures.

End on a high note.
- Express your appreciation for everyone's contributions and things that went well, for example, abiding by the rules or creating a win/win situation.

- Establish your willingness to meet again over unresolved issues or to check on progress.

After Conflict

Assess yourself.
- What did I do well?

- What areas still need improvement?

- Did I work to create win/win solutions?

- Was I respectful and courteous to everyone involved, particularly those whose ideas were rejected?

- How will others view me and my actions?

- If the conflict remains, is it due to a lack of effort on my part?

_____

_____

_____

_____

_____

_____

_____

_____

_____

_____

_____

_____

Seek feedback from trusted others.
- Did I make this a win/win situation for everyone?

- Was I sensitive to the other party and his/her needs?

- Did I employ Dynamic Listening and Dynamic Communication when needed?

_____

_____

_____

_____

_____

_____

_____

_____

Follow up with the person with whom you were in conflict.
- Express appreciation for his/her contribution to the problem-solving session.

- Meet periodically to discuss problems and head off potential conflicts before they develop.

If the conflict remains unresolved:
- Try again later when tensions are lower. Apologize for your role in the conflict and express regret at being unable to get it resolved during the earlier attempt.

- Changing the time, place, methods, etc. of the negotiations may help change negative patterns that have become established.

- Enlist a third party to serve as a go-between. This person should be impartial, neutral, and focused on reaching a mutually satisfactory solution.

- Hire a professional mediator or facilitator to resolve the conflict.

Motto: Confront conflict constructively.

_____

_____

_____

_____

_____

_____

_____

_____

_____

_____

_____

_____

_____

_____

_____

_____

_____

_____

Accepting Conflict

Successful management of conflict requires one final step. After attempts at conflict resolution have ended, either successfully or unsuccessfully, it is necessary to move on in as healthy and optimistic a way as possible. If the conflict has been resolved to everyone's satisfaction, this is relatively easy to do. Frequently, however, conflicts may be only temporarily or partially resolved, and hard feelings may persist. When this happens, the effective conflict manager must be able to cope with and accept what cannot be changed.

This section considers the aftermath of conflict and conflict resolution, particularly those situations where tension and stress remain. **Self-Appraisal** provides insight and advice for those who tend to doubt themselves or their ability to handle conflict. **Adapting** urges optimism, flexibility and integrity in those situations where conflict remains. Finally, **When Conflicts Can't be Resolved** poses questions and points to consider for those situations that have become intolerable. Accepting the inevitability of conflict in the workplace does not mean enduring it beyond your limits; it means coping with it as best you can and acknowledging those situations that should be left behind.

Top Tips For Accepting Conflict

1. Be self-confident, not self-critical.

2. Act professionally and ethically.

3. Adjust, adapt, improve.

4. Accentuate the positive.

5. Acknowledge that some conflicts can't be resolved.

SELF-APPRAISAL

Doubt whom you will, but never yourself.
                              Christine Bovee

Dynamic Example:

What for most people would be a minor conflict becomes for Marilyn a major problem. She blames herself for not having handled the situation better: "If only I had kept quiet. I was too forward. I shouldn't have said what I did." She sometimes made herself so upset by mentally replaying the incident that she would go home with headaches. Several days later, Marilyn would still be criticizing herself, but rather than learning from this instance and becoming less impulsive, she just fretted and worried.

Honest self-appraisal after a conflict can be an important motivation for change and therefore a constructive response to conflict. In fact, it is an integral part of the "After Conflict" advice offered throughout this guide. But when self-appraisal becomes overly negative self-criticism, then a potentially destructive response to conflict has emerged. The self-critical person repeatedly replays the incident over in his or her mind and fails to move on after the conflict has ended. Ignored is any contribution the other party made to the conflict, as is anything that might be used as the basis for self-improvement.

Self-criticism and the resulting distress and feelings of helplessness can impair judgement and decision-making as well as affect behavior. Personal and work relationships can suffer. A person who is too critical of him/herself may also be too critical or

demanding of others. The self-critical person may also perpetuate conflict and harm relationships by continually bringing up the conflict in repeated attempts to resolve it "perfectly." In addition, one's physical and emotional well-being can be affected. Hypertension, heart and respiratory problems, digestive ailments, sleep disorders, anxiety, depression, and panic attacks have all been linked to self-induced stress.

The causes of an overly critical or negative self-appraisal are complex, but often they are rooted in the unrealistically high standards one may set. When unable to reach their goals, some people are overly hard on themselves. They are also frequently inaccurate in their appraisals. Self-critical people tend to be selectively attentive to those cues that are negative or in line with their critical self-perceptions. They rarely acknowledge their skills or good points, and consequently, tend to have a negative view of themselves. In addition, a large discrepancy often exists between the self-critical person's perceptions and the perceptions of others. What others don't see at all or write off as minor mistakes or conflicts are blown all out of proportion or obsessed over by the self-critical. In short, a self-critical person — like the person who only blames others — fails to accurately perceive reality.

Honest and accurate self-appraisal, on the other hand, not only can motivate change but can also boost self-esteem, decrease stress, and enhance job performance. This is, however, not easy to accomplish. More than any other type of person described in ***Managing Conflict Dynamics***, the self-critical person needs to enlist others for support and guidance — trusted friends, honest co-workers, a patient mentor, and worthy role models. With their help and your own motivation, you can stop being your own worst enemy and become your own best friend.

Before Conflict

Begin with Reflection Questions.
- Is the conflict under examination worth the time and energy I'm spending on it?

- Do I appraise situations correctly?

- Which behaviors and situations trigger my self-criticism?

- Why do I *choose* to "beat myself up?"

- Am I aware of irrational thoughts, such as "I must have everyone like me," or "I must always succeed"?

- What have been the physical and emotional consequences of my self-criticism?

_____

_____

_____

_____

_____

_____

_____

_____

_____

_____

Conduct an honest appraisal of yourself, your abilities, and your behavior.
- Examine your goals and standards. Are they realistic?
- Enlist trusted co-workers or friends for their viewpoints.

- Compare your self-appraisal with those offered by others.

- Evaluate the discrepancies between viewpoints.
- Commit to bringing your self-appraisal more in line with that of others.

_____

_____

_____

_____

_____

_____

_____

_____

_____

_____

_____

Let valid criticism (yours and others') motivate change.
- Change your perceptions of yourself.

- Change your perceptions of others.

- Change the way you interact with others.

- Accept that which cannot be changed.

Pick a day on which you will write down each of your negative thoughts and words.
- Evaluate but don't magnify the negative.

- Practice positive thoughts and words.

- Envision how outcomes could be different if you changed negative thoughts into positive ones.

Put yourself and your problems in their proper perspective.
- Accentuate the positive; eliminate the negative (Harold Arlen).

- Don't sweat the small stuff (Richard Carlson).

- Be optimistic. If you think good things will happen, they will.

Commit to acting and thinking differently.
- Envision the "New You." Replay this vision in your mind until you are comfortable with it.

- Plan how to enact the "New You." Envision different scenarios and how you would handle each.

- Establish a support-and-guidance group: friends, co-workers, mentors, role models.

- Publicly commit to making changes. Tell others what you will do and when.

- Keep your goal clearly in focus.

Remind yourself:
- No one is perfect. Perfection isn't expected or required.

- If it can be changed, I will change it. If it can't be changed, I will forget about it.

- Setbacks will occur. I will be prepared for them.

During Conflict

Recognize potentially self-defeating, negative thoughts, words, and deeds. Replace them with positive words and constructive responses.
- I am productive and professional.

- I am a valuable member of this organization.

- I will not second-guess myself. I will stand by my actions and decisions.

Avoid linking your self-image to the conflict. Remember:
- It is impossible for everyone to like me.

- Even if others don't like me, they may like my ideas.

- Rejection of my ideas doesn't mean that others are rejecting me.

- Q-TIP — Quit Taking It Personally!

After Conflict

Assess yourself.
- What did I do well?

- What areas still need improvement?

- Did I assess the importance of the situation correctly?

- Did I change negative thoughts and responses to positive ones?

- Was I successful in separating my self-image from the conflict?

_____

_____

_____

_____

_____

_____

_____

_____

_____

_____

Seek feedback from trusted others.
- Was my behavior appropriate for the situation?

- Are my perceptions of what occurred and how I handled it accurate?

- Am I taking this conflict too personally?

_____

_____

_____

_____

_____

_____

_____

_____

_____

_____

_____

Accept yourself for who you are. Review Adapting (Page 74), especially these points:
- Live in the present, not the past.

- Do things that make you feel good about yourself.

- Learn to laugh at yourself. Take things less seriously.

- Appreciate yourself.

Continue to monitor self-critical thoughts and behaviors. Strive to replace them with positive, motivating ones.
- Accentuate the positive; eliminate the negative.

- Reframe "I'm not good enough," to "I am a productive and valuable member of this organization."

- Change "I can't do anything right," to "I can meet realistic expectations."

Problems affect people differently. What may not be a problem for some may be a serious one for others. Seek counseling from a competent professional if your self-criticism seems to be:
- Detrimental to your work.

- Interfering with personal relationships.

- Harmful to your health and well-being.

- Holding you back from being the person you want to be.

- Out of your control.

Motto:
Q-TIP
Quit Taking It Personally!

_____

_____

_____

_____

_____

_____

_____

_____

_____

_____

ADAPTING

Better little with content than much with contention.
                    Benjamin Franklin

Dynamic Example:

Several weeks after her argument with David, Sarah was still angry. Every time she thought about it (which was often), she got just as upset as the day it happened. Since so much time had passed, she was pessimistic about it ever being resolved, and her negativity was beginning to affect her work. In fact, she was so mired in hopelessness that she completely missed David's occasional friendly overtures and his efforts to move beyond their conflict.

By being adaptable in the face of conflict, an individual reacts by waiting to see if things improve while remaining flexible and hoping for the best. Adapting doesn't mean giving in or giving up. Rather, it means acknowledging that conflict on the job (and in life) is inevitable, while remaining hopeful that it is ultimately resolvable. Adaptability requires remaining alert for changing circumstances or cues signaling that the other party is ready to again try resolving the conflict. Optimism, flexibility, and a willingness to take advantage of opportunities for conflict resolution are all components of adaptability.

The consequences of not adapting can be far-reaching. Negativity and pessimism are not only detrimental to your work and relationships with co-workers, but can also carry over to your personal life and physical well-being. Most importantly, they may cause you to overlook or ignore opportunities for conflict resolution. Adapting is not always easy. It requires letting go of the past while remaining hopeful for the future. But with a positive attitude and a willingness to be flexible will come peace of mind and hopefully conflict resolution.

Before Conflict

Begin with Reflection Questions.
- Have I been flexible and optimistic?

- What have been the personal and professional consequences of not adapting?

- Do I take advantage of opportunities for conflict resolution when they present themselves?

- How do I want to be viewed when the conflict is over?

_____

_____

_____

_____

_____

_____

_____

_____

_____

_____

Think thoughts that lead you towards adapting and accepting.
- I will be positive and expect things to turn out well.

- I am willing to compromise.

- "Nothing can bring you peace but your self" (Ralph Waldo Emerson).

During Conflict

Remind yourself to:
- Look for the best in people and in the situation.

- Make concerted, sincere efforts to get along with others.

- Focus on the job, not personalities.

Act constructively.
- Be professional in your attitude, words, and behavior.

- Avoid sarcasm, cynicism, and negative or hostile humor.

- Express your willingness to continue working towards conflict resolution.

- Communicate your optimism that things will work out.

- Remain alert for opportunities for conflict resolution.

After Conflict

Assess yourself.
- What did I do well?

- What areas still need improvement?

- How will I continue to be adaptable?

- How will others view me and my actions?

_____

_____

_____

_____

_____

Seek feedback from trusted others.
- Have I been overlooking any opportunities for conflict resolution?

- Am I "rolling with the punches" and trying to stay positive?

_____

_____

_____

_____

_____

_____

_____

_____

_____

_____

Look forward, not back.
- Learn from your past accomplishments.

- Strive to change your present behavior.

- Work towards your future goals.

Don't let your job performance slide.
- Do your best work ever by putting in extra time and effort.

- Volunteer for new projects.

- Showcase your productivity.

- Maintain relationships with your co-workers and develop new ones.

Appreciate yourself. Praise or reward yourself when you:
- Achieve goals.

- Take risks.

- Learn something new.

- Meet challenges.

- Exceed expectations.

Increase your "emotional distance" from the job and the organization.
- Spend more time on your personal and family life.

- Engage in activities specifically aimed at relaxation, such as meditation, massage, or Tai Chi.

- Develop new and engaging outside interests or hobbies such as painting, gardening, collecting, learning a musical instrument, etc.

- Find comfort, support, and inspiration in reading. (Research shows that reading is more relaxing than watching TV.)

Retain (or cultivate) your sense of humor.
- Smile more!
- Look for the absurdities in situations.

- Start a collection of cartoons, comics, jokes, funny movies or TV shows that make you laugh. Review them frequently.

- Join in others' fun. Tell funny stories about yourself.

- Avoid sarcasm, cynicism, and negative or hostile humor.

Rely on others.
- Seek out sympathetic co-workers or friends when you need to "unload." Tell them when you need a pep talk.

- Turn to a more experienced person for advice or mentoring.

- Join a support group.

Tell yourself:
- I am hopeful that the conflict can still be resolved.

- I will look for indications that the time is right to try conflict resolution again.

- If I've done all I can, then that's all I can do.

- I will turn it loose and move on.

Follow up with the person with whom you were in conflict.
- If opportunities to reconcile or resolve the conflict arise, keep trying.

- Remain professional in your demeanor, words, and behavior.

Motto:
Nothing can bring
you peace but yourself.

WHEN CONFLICTS CAN'T BE RESOLVED

Accept with serenity the things that cannot be changed, courage to change the things which should be changed, and the wisdom to distinguish the one from the other.
Reinhold Niebuhr

Even when a conflict is rooted in fundamental differences in beliefs and values, a peaceful, productive relationship can be established. Unfortunately, however, some differences are irreconcilable. When a conflict cannot be resolved, the resulting situation can be detrimental to one's career as well as to one's physical and emotional well-being. It is then necessary to address some difficult issues.

Begin with Reflection Questions.
• How hard have I tried to correct the problem?

• Has every possible means of conflict resolution been tried?

• Can I live with this amount of conflict?

• Is this conflict serious enough to end the relationship?

• Is remaining in this situation damaging to any party or the organization?

• Do the positive aspects of this relationship or situation outweigh the negative ones?

• What are the personal and professional consequences of remaining here with the conflict unresolved?

• What are my alternatives both inside and outside of this organization?

_____

_____

_____

_____

_____

_____

_____

_____

Seek feedback from trusted others.
• Do I understand what is at the root of the conflict?

• Have I done everything I can do to resolve the conflict?

• Is remaining in this situation damaging to any party or the organization?

• What are my alternatives to remaining in this situation?

_____

_____

_____

_____

_____

_____

_____

_____

Have you tried everything you can to resolve the conflict?
- Let emotions cool before trying again.

- Taken the first step, listened, cooperated, created solutions.

- Apologized, apologized, apologized.

- Ascertained that you are not the main obstacle to conflict resolution.

- Repeatedly expressed your desire and willingness to continue working towards conflict resolution.

- Tried to resolve the conflict through writing as well as face-to-face.

- Changed the time, place, methods, etc. of the resolution process.

- Asked others to look at the conflict objectively and help search for solutions.

- Enlisted an impartial third party to serve as a go-between.

- Hired a professional mediator or facilitator.

Weigh the pros and cons of (1) remaining with vs. (2) leaving the organization. Consider such areas as:
- Your goals and career path.

- Your reputation.

- The financial and economic repercussions.

- Your personal and family life.

- Your emotional and physical well-being.

Motto: Know when to say when.

Chapter IV

Cooling Hot Buttons

Keep cool and you command everybody.

Louis de Saint-Just

Hot Buttons are those irritations and annoyances that can provoke you into conflict. They are the situations or characteristics in others that aggravate and frustrate you, perhaps to the point where, despite knowing better, you instigate a conflict. Interactions with button pushers can leave you feeling demoralized, unmotivated, powerless, anxious, frightened, and angry (possibly enough to resort to sabotage or other destructive acts). In the workplace, Hot Buttons can lead you to be less productive, efficient, organized, and creative; they can also negatively affect your life outside of work as well as your physical and emotional well-being.

With insight into what your Hot Buttons are, you can develop alternative "cool" reactions to button pushing. By taking the perspective of the button pushers, you can understand their motivations and actions. In addressing your reactions to button pushing and the pushers, you can confront conflict more effectively. By cooling your Hot Buttons as you attempt to influence button pushers, you can feel more in control of yourself and your work, have greater confidence, and fewer negative emotions. You can be a productive and successful member of your organization and feel as though the time and effort you put in are worthwhile.

Facing Reality

Developing insight and making behavioral changes won't come easily. They will require changing habitual reactions to provocation, responding to the button pushers with new tactics, and even interpreting actions and situations in alternative ways. The first step, however, in cooling your Hot Buttons is acknowledging some harsh realities and painful truths.

Reality #1: You're on your own. You're unlikely to get anything other than words of support and sympathetic pats from your co-workers. Similarly, don't expect help from your superiors or the organization, especially if the button pusher is effective on the job. (In fact, button-pushing behaviors such as micromanaging or being overly-analytical are expected and even rewarded in many organizations.) In short, you're on your own and the responsibility for change rests with you.

Reality #2: Your interpretation of the situation determines your reactions. Evaluating alternative ways of interpreting our world is not something we undertake routinely. But by becoming aware of how your perceptions can influence feelings and behavior, you can cool your Hot Buttons and respond more effectively. Consider, for example, a recent instance in which your Hot Button was pushed. Could the situation have been perceived in a different way? Are there alternative explanations for why the button pusher behaved as s/he did? Would your Hot Button have been pushed if you'd interpreted the situation differently? Most importantly, were your perceptions accurate? By questioning the accuracy of your perceptions, you may discover new ways of interpreting provocation and pushers.

Reality #3: Preventing button pushing requires determination, effort, and inconvenience. You may have to work at preventing your Hot Buttons from being pushed by doing things you really don't want to do. You may, for example, have to perform tasks that rightfully belong to an unreliable boss to ensure that they are done right and on time. You may even have to alter informal behaviors such as eating lunch in your office rather than socializing in the cafeteria with an abrasive and self-centered colleague.

Reality #4: Unless button pushers are willing to change, you can't change them. You can (and should) try, but your efforts may not work. You are, after all, trying to change someone who doesn't know or believe that change is needed. Attempt to modify a button pusher's behavior, but be prepared for less than completely successful outcomes.

Reality #5: Cooling your Hot Buttons has more to do with you than with the button pushers. This is the harshest reality of all. You can't change anything about others, but you can change everything about yourself: how you perceive button pushers, how you interpret their behaviors, what you feel about them and their actions, whether or not you're provoked, and most importantly, how you respond when provoked. You can't change the button pusher, so change how you feel.

Cooling Yourself

As revealed in Reality #5, the real secret to cooling your Hot Buttons is cooling yourself. Hot Buttons are, after all, those situations and personal characteristics in others that irritate, annoy, or frustrate you. It's your angry feelings and your negative thoughts that you let provoke you into conflict.

If you learn nothing else about Hot Buttons from this manual, learn this: ***You choose how you feel***. *You* control whether a Button is Hot or Cold. *You* control how you feel about others and their behavior. If, for example, you feel unmotivated working for an unappreciative boss, realize that you are choosing to feel unmotivated. If you get irritated while trying to collaborate with an aloof team member, remember that you are allowing yourself to be irritated. When your Buttons are pushed, you can get upset and blame the button pusher, or you can accept responsibility for feeling and acting in a different way. ***You can't change the button pusher, so change how you feel***. Don't let your negative emotions lead you into negative or destructive behavior. Take note of your co-workers who don't get upset by micro-managing bosses or a hostile co-worker; if they can take things in stride, *so can you*.

Cooling yourself also involves gaining some insight into your Hot Buttons. Does just one particular individual push your Button or is the problem more wide-spread? Is this a recent development or a long-standing issue? Most importantly, why are your Hot Buttons hot? Do you, for instance, have an unusually strong need for independence that's bound to clash with a micro-manager's style? Or does your desire for validation and approval mean that you'll be frustrated working for an unappreciative boss? Your hottest Hot Buttons, that is, the ones which are most irritating for you, will be the ones most likely to evoke quick and automatic destructive responses, while your cooler Buttons are more likely to result in a mixture of responses including some constructive behaviors. Your goal, therefore, is to learn to respond to the more provocative events in more constructive ways.

Contending with Button Pushers

One of the greatest challenges we encounter in life is trying to change the behavior of other people. Of course, it's not possible to completely change or control anyone much less a button pusher who thinks everyone else is the problem. (Ironically, while they can readily identify others who are problematic individuals, button pushers will seldom see those same characteristics in themselves.)

It is, however, possible to develop more effective ways of contending with button pushers by understanding a little more about their underlying motivations. The reasons for button pushers acting as they do are as varied as people themselves. Some lack skills; others lack knowledge. Some are unaware as to how they come across; others are aware but don't care. Some are just cruel individuals who enjoy tormenting people or demonstrating their power by frightening or manipulating others. Frequently, button pushers lack self-confidence or feel inadequate, and actions such as putting others down make them feel better about themselves.

Viewing the button pusher and the conflict situation from new and different perspectives can short-circuit the feeling that you are being provoked. Perceiving people and situations differently involves a bit of creativity since new perceptions involve generating a variety of options and choosing which of them best fits a logical analysis of the situation. Through a perspective-taking technique (see Page 26), you can hopefully gain insight into what drives button pushers and how they may be interpreting the situation.

Once you have considered things from the button pusher's perspective and have a better understanding of his/her motivations

and position, you can begin to confront the conflict constructively. If, for example, at the root of the button pusher's actions is distrust, jealousy, or dislike, strive to turn your foe into a friend. Praise those who need self-confidence. Confront those who are manipulative or untrustworthy. Refuse to be a helpless victim.

What follows on Pages 87-104 are strategies, guidelines, and tips for cooling any type of Hot Button before, during, and after conflict. Described on subsequent pages are nine common workplace Hot Buttons and advice for handling these specific problems.

Before Conflict

Begin with Reflection Questions.
- Why is this Button Hot for me rather than Cool?
- When my Hot Button is pushed, how do I usually feel? How do I usually respond?
- The next time my Hot Button is pushed, how do I want to feel? How do I want to respond?
- What environmental factors such as noise, heat, or crowds affect the triggering of my Hot Button(s)?
- What have been the personal and professional consequences of responding as I do to my Hot Button(s)?

_____

_____

_____

_____

Analyze a specific instance in which the pushing of your Hot Button(s) provoked conflict.
- When, where, and how did the situation arise? What happened?

- How did I feel? Were my feelings justified by the situation?

- How did I react? Were my actions justified by the situation?

- Did my actions serve to escalate my emotions or the conflict?

- In what alternative ways could I have reacted to the provocation?

- Could this situation have been perceived in a different way?

- Would my Hot Buttons have been pushed if I'd taken a different view of the situation?

_____

_____

_____

_____

_____

_____

Try to understand the button pusher. Use the perspective-taking technique described in Dynamic Listening (Page 25) to answer these questions:
- Does the button pusher behave this way only towards me? If so, why?

- Is this a new, temporary way of behaving or a long-standing characteristic?

- Why might the button pusher be acting this way? What does s/he gain?

- Does the button pusher know what I expect?

- Does the button pusher have the skills, abilities, or resources to act in a different manner or reach my expectations?

- Does the button pusher have incentives to act in a different manner?

- In what alternative ways do I want the button pusher to behave?

_____

_____

_____

_____

_____

_____

_____

_____

_____

Reflect on others' ways of dealing with button pushers.
- What methods are successful?

- What methods are unsuccessful?

- How do they cope with the emotional strain that results from interacting with button pushers?

_____

_____

_____

_____

_____

_____

_____

Envision your next encounter with the button pusher and how you could handle it.

- Think through all the options.

- Imagine each option played out, especially the worst-case scenario.

- Evaluate the pros and cons of each.

- Determine how to put the best option into effect.

Accentuate the positive. Focus on what the button pusher can do *for* you rather than *to* you.

- The overly-analytical can teach you organizational and analytical skills.

- The micro-manager can train you for higher management positions.

- The self-centered frequently impart useful knowledge and information.

- The aloof and unappreciative encourage independence and self-sufficiency.

- The abrasive can often quickly identify problems and obstacles.

If possible, exclude button pushers from your projects.

- Offer tactful ways for them to "bow out."

- Pledge to keep them informed as necessary. Keep your promise.

Tell yourself:

- I control whether a Button is Hot or Cold.

- I control how I respond when my Button is pushed.

- Attack the problem, not the pusher.

- I will channel my negative emotions in a positive direction.

During Conflict

Get started by Taking Action (Page 56), especially these points:

- View obstacles as challenges.

- Tackle more easily-resolved problems and issues first.

- Ask what you can do to improve the relationship. *Listen* to the answer.

Be a role model.

- Be optimistic and approachable.

- Treat people with sensitivity, fairness, and respect.

- Don't be manipulative, distrustful, judgmental, or defensive.

- Keep your emotions in check. Remember: If you lose it, you lose.

Use principles of Dynamic Communication (Page 29), especially these points:

- TLC — Think, Listen, Communicate.

- Make your points in a non-threatening way.

- Stop frequently to make sure the other person understands you.

- Be alert to signs of resistance to what you are saying.

- Be very careful in your use of humor.

Convince them with kindness. The more hostile, abrasive, unreliable, etc. the button pushers are, the nicer you will be.

- Speak in a soothing, calm voice.

- Express friendliness and kindness.

- Maintain a receptive facial expression.

- Smile.

- Counter their insecurities with understanding and esteem-boosters.

- Mention their strengths and good points (they must have some!).

Directly, but privately and tactfully, confront the button pusher about his/her behavior. Review Criticizing Constructively (Page 34), especially these points:

- Explain that your goal is professional—to improve your productivity as well as the organization's functioning and environment.

- Emphasize your feelings, the consequences for your work, and the organization's functioning rather than attacking the button pusher.

- Describe as specifically as possible your expectations for a different way of behaving.

- Use statements that begin with "I" rather than "You," for example, "I feel angry when you demean me. It makes me not want to do my best work for you."

- Balance negative statements with compliments and appreciation.

Use a "mirroring" technique to reflect back to the button pusher how his/her behavior looks. This tactic can be especially effective when combined with humor (if appropriate). For example:

- To a micro-manager: "And do you also want to tell me what to eat for lunch?"

- To an aloof person: "Same time, next year?"

- To an unappreciative boss: "It may look as though I'm fishing for compliments, and I am! Are you pleased with the work I'm doing?"

Remember that *you are feeling what you choose to feel*. Resolve to think and feel differently.
- Choose to chill. Do not let yourself be irritated or annoyed.

- Re-define the situation as ordinary workplace conflict.
- View each interaction as an opportunity to learn why the button pusher acts as s/he does and why you react as you do.

Manage the emotions that arise — theirs as well as yours.
- Temporarily distance yourself from a distressing situation (Taking Time Outs, Page 39).

- Get control of your most destructive emotions (Controlling Anger, Page 43).

- Explain to the button pusher's how his/her actions make you feel and the consequences of that for your work and the organization's functioning (Expressing Emotions, Page 51).

- If you are responsible for provoking the button pusher's actions, apologize or otherwise make amends (Reaching Out, Page 47).

After Conflict

Assess yourself.
- What did I do well?

- How did I feel when my Hot Button was pushed? How did I react?

- Did I make progress towards changing the button pusher's behavior?

- How will others view me and my actions?

- If the conflict remains unresolved, it is due to my Hot Button(s)?

_____

_____

_____

_____

_____

_____

_____

_____

_____

_____

_____

Seek feedback from trusted others.

• Did I handle myself in a constructive, professional manner?

• Did I interpret the situation accurately?

• In what alternative ways could I have responded?

_____

_____

_____

_____

_____

_____

_____

_____

_____

If your efforts at changing the button pusher's behavior seem to be successful (and if appropriate for the situation):

• Praise every improvement, no matter how small.

• Emphasize the benefits of continuing to change.

If your Hot Buttons are still hot or conflict remains:

• Cool down (way down) before trying again to resolve it.

• Change the time, place, methods, etc. of the resolution process.

• Enlist a fair and impartial third party to serve as a go-between.

• Choose to view the situation differently.

To help with your ability to cope with your Hot Buttons and button pushers, see Adapting (Page 74), especially these points:

• Be flexible and optimistic.

• Don't let your job performance slide. In fact, improve it.

• Appreciate and reward yourself.

• Keep your sense of humor.

Keep a paper trail and logbook documenting interactions (both good and bad) with the button pusher.

• When and where did the incident(s) occur?

• What was said and done by each party?

• Who else was around or witnessed the incident?

• Are there any relevant supporting documents or paperwork?

If it becomes necessary to inform your superiors, first consider:

- How supportive are they likely to be of your complaints?

- What could happen if this matter is not handled confidentially?

- Do others in the organization share your view of the button pusher? Will they support you in making a complaint?

- How might this affect your position, reputation, advancement, or career goals?

- What is the worst that could happen? Are you prepared for that possibility?

_____

_____

_____

_____

_____

_____

_____

_____

_____

_____

_____

_____

_____

In presenting your complaint:

- Don't whine. Be direct, forthright, and speak with confidence. Review Dynamic Communication (Page 29).

- Emphasize that you don't want to make trouble. You want to do a better job for the organization by being more effective and productive.

- Be objective and focus on the problematic situation, rather than the person.

- Explain how you have tried to solve this problem on your own. Provide documentation if you have it.

- Be specific and realistic about what you want to see happen. Have some suggestions ready to present. Emphasize that you want to be part of the solution.

Motto:
Choose to chill.

_____

_____

_____

_____

_____

_____

_____

_____

_____

_____

_____

_____

_____

_____

_____

_____

ABRASIVE

Rude am I in my speech, and little blessed with the soft phrase of peace.

Shakespeare (Othello)

Abrasive people have an unpleasant interpersonal style, and their lack of social skills often results in rude or curt interactions. Abrasive individuals are undiplomatic, insensitive to others, and have an arrogant attitude that can make contact with them quite demoralizing. Through sarcasm and insults disguised as "humor" or "constructive criticism," they ridicule, blame, and put other people on the defensive. An abrasive person may even be able to goad others into doing something they will regret.

Abrasive people may also tend to be pessimistic and discouraging. While their negativity can be contagious, it also has a benefit: abrasive people can often quickly and accurately identify problems and obstacles. While they may, unfortunately, focus on problems to the exclusion of solutions, they have a skill not to be overlooked in today's workplace.

Cooling Strategies

Begin with Reflection Questions.
- Why is the abrasive Button Hot for me rather than Cool?

- The next time my abrasive Hot Button is pushed, how do I want to feel? How do I want to respond?

- Why might the abrasive person be acting this way (self-doubt, insecurity, a need to be liked or admired, anger, frustration, etc.)?

- In what alternative ways do I want the abrasive button pusher to behave?

- Given my understanding of my abrasive Hot Button and the button pusher, which Cooling Strategies would be most useful?

_____

_____

_____

_____

_____

_____

_____

_____

_____

_____

_____

_____

Look beyond the abrasive style and examine the substance.
- Analyze their messages. Are their criticisms valid or important?

- Ask trusted others about the validity of the abrasive person's criticisms.

- View valid criticisms as constructive feedback and make the necessary changes.

Refuse to be a victim. Directly address the abrasive behavior or remarks.
- "I may well be wrong. Let's examine the facts."

- "Calling each other names is counterproductive. Let's focus on the issues."

- "That's not funny; it's hurtful. I can take a joke but not meanness."

- "Rather than assigning blame, let's brainstorm about how to solve the problem."

- "Do I understand from the expression on your face that you disagree with me?"

The negativity or pessimism associated with abrasive people can be contagious. To avoid it:

- Remember with whom you're dealing. They're the ones with the problem, not you.

- Acknowledge their point of view. Don't say, "You're wrong." (They may not be!)

- Counter their negative comments with optimism or humor.

- Invite discussion and creative problem-solving.

Be a role model.

- Consider others and their points of view.

- Be optimistic and encouraging.

- Never express cynicism or sarcasm.

> ### *Dynamic Fact:*
> Nearly 75% of those surveyed in our research said they were moderately to extremely upset when working with someone who is abrasive.

ALOOF

The worst sin toward our fellow creatures is not to hate them, but to be indifferent to them; that's the essence of inhumanity.
George Bernard Shaw

Those who are aloof isolate themselves, do not seek outside input, and are not open with others. They are detached and distant. Communication with an aloof person tends to be formal and sparse. When an aloof manager delegates tasks, for instance, s/he may do so without providing enough guidance as to what to do, how and when to do it, and within what limits.

Aloof individuals' "hands-off" style may also result in a lack of feedback regarding performance, and this can leave people with a great deal of uncertainty about where they stand and whether their work is acceptable. This style can also, however, be beneficial, in that it encourages independence and self-sufficiency. Take advantage of your freedom from oversight and guidance; become self-reliant.

Cooling Strategies

Begin with Reflection Questions.
• Why is the aloof Button Hot for me rather than Cool?

• The next time my aloof Hot Button is pushed, how do I want to feel? How do I want to respond?
• Why might the aloof person be acting this

way (shyness, anxiety, hostility, self-doubt, places a high value on self-reliance and independence, etc.)?

• In what alternative ways do I want the aloof button pusher to behave?

• Given my understanding of my aloof Hot Button and the button pusher, which Cooling Strategies would be most useful?

_____
_____
_____
_____
_____
_____
_____
_____
_____
_____
_____

In a non-accusatory yet direct way, tell aloof individuals you *want* more contact with them.
• Explain that their help will allow you to do a better job.

• Be specific about what you want (weekly planning sessions, delineation of your authority, increased supervision, etc.).

• Be specific about how this will help you, them, and the organization.

Emphasize that you:
• Value their knowledge and experiences.

• Sincerely want their opinions, insights, and guidance.

Encourage participation in discussions by asking open-ended questions such as:
- "What's your opinion?"

- "How do you view the task ahead of us?"

- "What problems do you foresee?"

Counteract an aloof person's attempts to postpone an issue or problem.
- Acknowledge his/her feelings: "I know this may be uncomfortable for you, but we can't ignore the problem any longer."

- Stand your ground. Firmly state: "We need to resolve this right now."

Make an effort to get to know the aloof person.
- Start small. Greet them with a smile and a friendly "How are you today?" Listen to the answer.

- Make small talk at a time and place that will be comfortable for them.

- Ask about their families and hobbies. Be interested and friendly, not intrusive.

Be a role model.
- Foster an atmosphere of open communication.

- Offer your opinions, insights, and guidance.

- Get to know your co-workers.

Dynamic Fact:

According to our research, those who are irritated by aloof co-workers tend to be viewed by their peers as more likely to engage in Destructive conflict responses and less likely to engage in Constructive ones.

HOSTILE

Anger is a short madness.
                    Horace

Hostile individuals are one of the most difficult types of people to contend with. Such people lose their tempers, throw tantrums, scream, swear, and otherwise act in angry and aggressive ways. A hostile person may frequently experience impatience with others and subsequently exhibit anger at the slightest provocation. Targets, as well as others within range, can quickly feel overwhelmed, afraid, and powerless.

Dealing with a hostile colleague can be an intimidating experience and you may feel as though you are constantly on guard so that you don't set the person off. Nonetheless, reacting in a non-angry manner to the hostile person is extremely important. Even though you may feel justified, losing your temper and engaging in a shouting match will do nothing but create more hostility, negativity, and conflict. Choose instead to create a calm, positive atmosphere.

Cooling Strategies

Begin with Reflection Questions.
• Why is the hostile Button Hot for me rather than Cool?

• The next time my hostile Hot Button is pushed, how do I want to feel? How do I want to respond?

• Why might the hostile person be acting this way (anxiety, self-doubt, high need for control, low tolerance for errors, etc.)?

• In what alternative ways do I want the hostile button pusher to behave?

• Given my understanding of my hostile Hot Button and the button pusher, which Cooling Strategies would be most useful?

_____

_____

_____

_____

_____

_____

_____

_____

_____

_____

_____

Avoid triggering hostile outbursts.
• Ascertain what *their* Hot Buttons are (e.g., latecomers to meetings, unreturned phone calls, personal problems interfering with work).

• Avoid pushing their Hot Buttons.

• If you can't avoid pushing their Buttons, warn them in advance whenever possible and apologize for not meeting their expectations.

When a hostile outburst occurs, ride it out.
• Act unafraid and in control.

• Sit or stand up straight. Look him/her in the eye.

• Control any anger you may be feeling (see Controlling Anger, Page 43).

- Ascertain if you are the cause of the outburst or the scapegoat for a problem caused by someone else.

- Don't respond until things are calmer.

When the hostile outburst has somewhat subsided, strive to cover the same ground in a calmer, more rational manner.
- Don't be defensive or accusatory. Say: "I'm sorry I've disappointed you. I certainly want to do better. Let's discuss calmly and specifically your concerns."

- Calmly repeat what you believe the hostile person is saying (see Dynamic Communication, Page 29).

- To show you're sincerely interested in the content of the message, take notes.

- Explain how the outburst affected you emotionally.

To avoid triggering additional outbursts during this time:
- Don't contradict a hostile person ("You're wrong; that will never work").

- Don't pass judgement ("That's a terrible idea").

- Present alternative viewpoints directly yet tactfully, such as "And here's a few other ideas," or "I disagree; in my opinion . . . ."

- If interrupted, firmly state: "You interrupted me," then continue.

If the outburst doesn't seem to be stopping, change the flow of the situation. For example:
- Drop your pencil and pick it up.

- Move to a different chair.

- Politely excuse yourself and leave the room (see Taking Time Outs, Page 39).

After some time has passed (hours or perhaps a few days), approach the hostile person.
- Acknowledge his/her good points and strengths.

- Describe the effects of his/her anger on you and others (demoralized, distressed, angry, etc.)

- Explain that you want to know when there's a problem but "Is there another way that your concerns could be expressed?"

- If appropriate, explore why the hostile outburst occurred: "Why is this minor problem upsetting you so much?"

Be a role model.
- Never scream, swear, rage, throw objects, or otherwise inappropriately display anger.

- Discuss your anger in a calm, informative manner.

- Take timeouts when angry and encourage others to do so.

> ### *Dynamic Fact:*
> Our research finds that people with a hostile Hot Button tend to respond to conflict by taking time outs.

MICRO-MANAGING

*We should manage this matter
to a T.*

Lawrence Stern

People who micro-manage continually check up on others and too closely monitor others' work. They may, for example, try to orchestrate every move, verify all calculations, or examine each piece of paperwork. Micro-managers may be excessively anxious about deadlines, budgets, progress, and perfection. The result is that colleagues and subordinates feel as though their work and decisions cannot be trusted and that their contributions are insignificant.

Working with a micro-managing person can be difficult and frustrating, particularly if your style is one of independence. But if you are trustworthy, competent and efficient, you should be able to convince the micro-manager of your abilities and gain his/her trust.

Cooling Strategies

Begin with Reflection Questions.
- Why is the micro-managing Button Hot for me rather than Cool?

- The next time my micro-managing Hot Button is pushed, how do I want to feel? How do I want to respond?

- Why might the micro-manager be acting this way (organizational policy or expectation, poor management training, high need for control, lacks confidence in others, etc.)?

- Have I contributed to making this person a micro-manager (producing sloppy or error-filled work, missing deadlines, etc.)?

- In what alternative ways do I want the micro-manager to behave?

- Given my understanding of my micro-managing Hot Button and the button pusher, which Cooling Strategies would be most useful?

_____

_____

_____

_____

_____

_____

_____

_____

_____

_____

_____

Openly discuss the micro-manager's view of your work (particularly if s/he micro-manages you and not others).

- Explain that you sincerely want to improve and be viewed as trustworthy.

- Ask: "What concerns do you have about my work? What else?"

- Listen attentively, not defensively. Take notes.

- Establish specifically what you need to do and when in order for the micro-manager to trust you. Then do it.

Request frequent monitoring and close

inspection to show that:
- You sincerely want to improve.

- Your goal is to be seen as trustworthy and competent.

- You have nothing to hide.

- The micro-manager has nothing to fear.

Take small steps towards gaining the micro-manager's trust.
- Meet or beat all deadlines.

- Have a trusted friend or co-worker check your work for errors or typos.

- Suggest a short period of low monitoring during which you will work on your own for a time before bringing your work to the micro-manager for feedback.

- Request a small portion of a large project as a test.
- Remind the micro-manager that your goal is to make both of you, as well as the organization, look good.

Be a role model.
- Trust others' abilities, skills, and decisions.

- Encourage independence and self-sufficiency.

- Take (or re-take) management training classes.

Dynamic Fact:

The surveys we conducted indicate that people whose Hot Button is micro-management are less likely to work at creating solutions to conflict.

OVERLY-ANALYTICAL

*A man may dwell so long
upon a thought that it may take
him prisoner.*

Lord Halifax

Overly-analytical people "can't see the forest for the trees." By focusing too much on minor issues, they often miss the "big picture." They are excessively concerned with details and may perform an in-depth analysis before undertaking even the most routine task. When making decisions, overly-analytical individuals painstakingly gather facts, analyze every potential outcome, and methodically deliberate pros and cons. Often, this process takes too much time, and others are kept waiting, resulting in unreasonable delays.

Overly-analytical people value order, thoroughness, and accuracy; indeed, these are likely to be precisely the qualities that have gotten them where they are today. Consequently, an overly-analytical colleague is exactly the right person to teach you organizational and analytical skills, project management, and thoughtful decision-making. While you will, of course, want to avoid the "hyper-conscientious" trap, these are skills that are valuable in any organization and well worth learning.

Cooling Strategies

Begin with Reflection Questions.
• Why is the overly-analytical Button Hot for me rather than Cool?

• The next time my overly-analytical Hot Button is pushed, how do I want to feel? How do I want to respond?

• Why might the overly-analytical person be acting this way (perfectionist, high need for control, fearful of making mistakes, lacks confidence in others, etc.)?

• Have I contributed to making this person overly-analytical (not paying attention to details, impulsive decision-making, poor planning, etc.)?

• In what alternative ways do I want the overly-analytical button pusher to behave?

• Given my understanding of my overly-analytical Hot Button and the button pusher, which Cooling Strategies would be most useful?

_____

_____

_____

_____

_____

_____

_____

_____

_____

_____

_____

Recognize that:
- You prefer the big picture to the details.

- Your big-picture style complements another person's overly-analytical style.

- Both styles have their advantages and disadvantages.

Prove that you are productive, efficient, and reliable.
- Do your work well. Put in extra time if necessary.

- Have a trusted friend or co-worker check your work for errors or typos.

- Exceed expectations by getting work in before deadlines and under budget.

- Showcase your efforts and abilities.

Reassure the overly-analytical person who seems particularly concerned about mistakes.
- Identify potential problems or obstacles and some means of preventing them.

- Present a backup plan in case things don't go as desired.
- Emphasize that if mistakes occur, you both will analyze and learn from them.
- Remind him/her that your goal is to make both of you, as well as the organization, look good.

Ease the overly-analytical person's decision-making process.
- Eliminate or reduce distractions (close the door, turn off background music, hold all phone calls).

- Provide choices. Ask, for example, "Should we do X or Y?" rather than "What should we do?"

- Prepare in advance your own list of options and their pros and cons. Be ready to present them when the time is right.

- Offer to assist with research, interviewing, or handling details of the decision-making process.

- Set firm deadlines.

Be a role model.
- Consider the details as well as the big picture.

- Trust others' skills, abilities, and decisions.

- Encourage learning from mistakes, rather than fearing them.

Dynamic Fact:
Our research finds that overly-analytical is the "coolest" (that is, least upsetting) Hot Button in the workplace.

SELF-CENTERED

Egotists do not see the world with themselves in it, but see themselves with the world around them.
Herbert Samuel

People who are self-centered believe they are always correct, act like "know-it-alls," and generally put themselves first. Given their focus on themselves, self-centered individuals may be quite insensitive to others. They may not recognize that others need or desire to participate. They may be unaware that their belief that they are always correct implies that others are always wrong, and that such an attitude can be hurtful or insulting.

While frustrating to work with, there is one potential benefit to being around the self-centered. Because they do often know a lot and share their knowledge so readily, you can learn much from them. Take what you can get.

Cooling Strategies

Begin with Reflection Questions.
- Why is the self-centered Button Hot for me rather than Cool?

- The next time my self-centered Hot Button is pushed, how do I want to feel? How do I want to respond?

- Why might the self-centered person be acting this way (anxiety, insecurity, self-doubt, etc.)?

- In what alternative ways do I want the self-centered button pusher to behave?

- Given my understanding of my self-centered Hot Button and the button pusher, which Cooling Strategies would be most useful?

_____
_____
_____
_____
_____
_____
_____
_____
_____
_____
_____
_____

Make self-centered individuals more amenable to others' input.
- Acknowledge their experience and insight.
- Express appreciation for their willingness to share information and teach others.
- Seek their advice occasionally.

Don't be a victim.
- Do your homework. Be prepared and knowledgeable.
- Request they share recognition. Highlight the benefits for everyone by doing so.
- When necessary, showcase your productivty and contributions.

When self-centered colleagues are wrong:
- Do not directly refute what they say, as that might be seen as a challenge.

• Use questions to lead them to discover problems or flaws in their plan.

If a self-centered person's insensitivity is hurtful or interfering with your ability to participate, calmly yet directly address the problem.
• Acknowledge his/her input and insight.

• Emphasize that you wish to contribute.

• If interrupted, firmly state: "You interrupted me," then continue.

Be a role model.
• Put others first.

• Listen more than you talk.

• Be encouraging and supportive of others.

Dynamic Fact:

According to our research, people with a self-centered Hot Button tend to respond to conflict by displaying anger and demeaning others.

UNAPPRECIATIVE

*The best definition of man is:
an ungrateful biped.*
                    Fedor Dostoevski

One of the most distressing situations in the workplace is dealing with people who are unappreciative of others. Such people fail to praise, reward effort, or offer encouragement. In their view, workers are doing what they should be doing and therefore don't require gratitude. Some unappreciative people may even go in the other direction and become overly critical. While their intention may be to motivate better job performance, what they might not understand is that people need praise, attention, and recognition to do their jobs well.

It is difficult to gain an understanding of the quality of your work and your place in the organization when you receive little recognition, few rewards, and no praise. One attribute you might be gaining, though, is self-sufficiency and independence. No one knows better than you what your work and efforts have been. Rely on yourself for your rewards.

Cooling Strategies

Begin with Reflection Questions.
- Why is the unappreciative Button Hot for me rather than Cool?

- The next time my unappreciative Hot Button is pushed, how do I want to feel? How do I want to respond?

- Why might the unappreciative person be acting this way (unaware of importance of appreciation, feels gratitude is unnecessary, unreasonably high expectations, etc.)?

- Have my efforts and contributions to this organization been worthy of praise, rewards, and appreciation?

- In what alternative ways do I want the unappreciative button pusher to behave?

- Given my understanding of my unappreciative Hot Button and the button pusher, which Cooling Strategies would be most useful?

_____

_____

_____

_____

_____

_____

_____

_____

_____

_____

Explain that an expression of appreciation:
- Is important to you.

- Aids you in measuring your progress.

- Motivates you to improve.

Look beyond the unappreciative person.
- Start a "Mutual Admiration Society." Develop a network of co-workers who reward and appreciate each other.

• Suggest organizational-level rewards, such as an "Employee of the Month" parking space.

"If you can't get a compliment any other way, pay yourself one" (Mark Twain). Appreciate and reward yourself when you:

• Achieve goals.

• Take risks.

• Learn something new.

• Meet challenges.

• Exceed expectations.

Be a role model.
• Reward hard work.

• Acknowledge loyalty.

• Express gratitude for effort.

Dynamic Fact:
Over 60% of those we surveyed said they were moderately to extremely upset when working with someone who does not reward hard work.

UNRELIABLE

A wrongdoer is often a man who has left something undone, not always one who has done something.

Marcus Aurelius

One of the most frustrating types of people to work with is those who are unreliable. They make commitments but don't follow through, and cannot be counted on to get work done. They procrastinate, miss deadlines, lack organization, and don't take crises seriously. Unreliable people may also impulsively make decisions without first checking with others, then find that they lack the necessary support from co-workers or superiors. Because their unreliability affects everyone with whom they work, they can be quite detrimental to an organization's functioning.

The easiest type of unreliable co-worker to help is one who is unorganized, has poor time management skills, or doesn't know how to set goals, priorities, or timetables. Any time you take to teach organizational or time-management skills will pay off. Not only will making this person more reliable help you to be more productive and less anxious, but displaying your skills and your willingness to help others will reflect well on you.

Cooling Strategies

Begin with Reflection Questions.
• Why is the unreliable Button Hot for me rather than Cool?

• The next time my unreliable Hot Button is pushed, how do I want to feel? How do I want to respond?

• Why might the unreliable person be acting this way (indecisive, doesn't know how to get started or make progress, unorganized, poor time management, insecurity, etc.)?

• In what alternative ways do I want the unreliable button pusher to behave?

• Given my understanding of my unreliable Hot Button and the button pusher, which Cooling Strategies would be most useful?

_____

_____

_____

_____

_____

_____

_____

_____

_____

_____

Offer to help with time and project management.
• Establish priorities and goals. Keep goals small and limited at first.

• Set early and frequent deadlines.

• Discuss organization of projects, files, desktop, calendar, etc.

• Stress the importance of returning phone calls, responding to memos, making daily to-do lists, etc.

- Recommend a particular book or course on project or time management.

Bring indecisiveness out into the open.
- "Having a problem getting started?"

- "What are our options? Let's brainstorm to get things going."

- "Let's approach this systematically. What needs to be done first?"

Be supportive and encouraging.
- "You're making good progress."

- "You've got us all on the right path."

- "Good decision. Even though it didn't go my way, I still like you."

Don't:
- Push too hard.

- Annoy, pester, or nag.

- Go over their heads.

- Usurp their authority.

- Appear self-serving.

Protect yourself.
- "Never depend on the other fellow for he may be depending on you" (Anonymous).

- Keep the unreliable out of the loop.

- Avail yourself of what they are able to provide, perhaps information, advice, or feedback.

- Delegate their work to others, or encourage them to delegate their tasks.

Be a role model.
- Act thoughtfully and decisively.

- Follow through on your commitments.

- Improve your organizational and time-management skills.

Dynamic Fact:
The only Hot Button showing significant gender differences is Unreliable - females get more upset than males when working with someone who is unreliable.

UNTRUSTWORTHY

The louder he talked of his honor, the faster we counted our spoons.

Ralph Waldo Emerson

Untrustworthy people are exploitative, manipulative, and dishonest. They use other people for their own purposes and may be quite willing to deceive and cheat. They may try to undercut colleagues, or deliberately sabotage others' work by, for instance, keeping important information to themselves. They may attempt to take credit for others' successes.

Either deliberately or indirectly, untrustworthy individuals undermine others' efforts, success, authority, and feelings of self-worth. Clearly, untrustworthy people lack not only honesty and ethics, but also compassion and empathy.

Cooling Strategies

Begin with Reflection Questions.
- Why is the untrustworthy Button Hot for me rather than Cool?

- The next time my untrustworthy Hot Button is pushed, how do I want to feel? How do I want to respond?

- Why might the untrustworthy person be acting this way (angry, envious, lacks self-confidence, anxious, lacks integrity, etc.)?

- In what alternative ways do I want the untrustworthy button pusher to behave?

- Given my understanding of my untrustworthy Hot Button and the button pusher, which Cooling Strategies would be most useful?

_____

_____

_____

_____

_____

_____

_____

Clarify the situation by distinguishing among types of dishonesty. Are the dishonest acts:
- Intentionally or unintentionally committed?

- Acts of omission or commission?

- Major or minor breaches of trust?

- Violations of your personal moral code or ethical standards?

- Violations of the organization's code of ethics?

- Illegal or quasi-illegal actions?

Assess:
- Who is being harmed (you, others, the organization, community or society)?

- In what ways?

- Why or for what ends?

- How problematic, unethical, or offensive is the behavior?

Ascertain whether *you* somehow initially caused trust to be broken. If so:
- Acknowledge and explain.

- Apologize and ask for forgiveness.

- Promise that it won't happen again.

- Keep your promise; be honest, fair, and ethical.

- Recognize that while trust can be destroyed with a single act, it grows back slowly. Be patient; this process is likely to require repeated efforts.

Confront an untrustworthy person in as non-accusatory way as possible by calmly explaining:

- Your goal is to stop unwanted behavior, not to punish, insult, or offend.

- You believe your values were violated, and you feel hurt and used.

- While you value him/her as a person and a co-worker, such behavior is not acceptable and will not be tolerated.

- You, as well as the organization, require honesty, fairness, integrity, and credibility.

Protect yourself.

- "The best armor is to keep out of range" (Italian proverb).

- Be wary and aware.

- Resist becoming involved in others' unethical activities.

- Listen for hidden messages, particularly in comments intended to be humorous.

- Keep all interactions limited and conducted as much as possible via written means.

- Don't work alone. Involve others as witnesses and project partners.

- Keep a logbook and document everything. Store these notes off-site.

- Be sure the necessary people, particularly your superiors, are aware of your efforts, contributions, ideas, the status of your projects, etc. Notify them yourself rather than relying on possibly untrustworthy others.

Because of the seriousness (and potential liability) of charging someone with dishonest or unethical behavior, be very certain of your case before informing your superiors (see page 86). In particular, consider:

- What are the costs to you if you take action?

- Is there a practical alternative?

- Do others share your assessment? Would they support you in a complaint?

Create an atmosphere of honesty, openness, and integrity.

- Acknowledge that rules, regulations, structure, and control can often be replaced with trust.

- Give trust and loyalty to gain trust and loyalty. Empower others to lead, make decisions, etc.

- Be forgiving (but not naïve). Allow second chances.

- Be sure you and others understand and abide by the organization's code of ethics and standards of integrity.

- If the organization doesn't have a code of ethics, volunteer to help establish one.

Be a role model.

- Act with honesty and integrity.

- Endorse and live by a strong code of personal and organizational ethics.

- Showcase and reward others for their work, efforts, and integrity.

Dynamic Fact:

Our research finds that for everyone in the workplace — male, female, manager or subordinate — the hottest (most upsetting) Hot Button in the workplace is untrustworthiness.

Chapter 5

Final Thoughts & Encouragement

Managing Conflict Dynamics: A Practical Approach has had one main theme: **while conflict is inevitable, ineffective and harmful responses to conflict can be avoided, and effective and beneficial responses to conflict can be learned.** With constructive methods of responding, not only can conflicts be resolved, but tensions can be reduced, relationships improved, productivity and creativity heightened. Through cooling your Hot Buttons and being attentive to others, conflicts can often be prevented from ever happening in the first place.

Our goal has been to change how you view conflict and to prepare you to manage it constructively and successfully. We hope that you will now not only be able to resolve your own conflicts, but that over time you will become someone who can mediate others' disputes and even coach colleagues in the techniques of conflict management. We wish to leave you with just a few final encouraging words . . . .

Encouragement #1: Conflict management is a skill. And like carpentry, tennis or any other skill, conflict management is learned. Destructive methods and bad habits can be unlearned, while mediocre techniques can be improved.

- Learning new skills will take time, effort, and perseverance. Changes will not occur overnight, no matter how motivated you are. Anticipate some slow-going as you learn and refine your new skills.

- Involve others in your learning. Ask for advice. Seek out mentors and role models. Continue to get feedback.

- Practice, practice, practice. Fortunately (or actually unfortunately) in today's world, there will be no shortage of opportunities in which to practice your conflict management skills.

Encouragement #2: Knowing what provokes conflict can prevent it from starting. Be attentive to those factors and situations that cause irritation, anxiety, and tension:

- Your Hot Buttons and the people who push them.

- Others' Hot Buttons, their job or personal problems, concerns and fears.

Encouragement #3: Changing how you manage conflict is within your grasp. You <u>can</u> do this!

- Following on page 107 is a handy, concise chart of some of the advice and tips described in this guide. Tape it to your bathroom mirror, office bulletin board, or somewhere where you will see it every day. Review it daily for encouragement and motivation.

- Get going, and remember: "Nothing is particularly hard if you divide it into small jobs" (Henry Ford).

- Persevere, and "Be grateful for luck but don't depend on it" (William Feather).

For additional encouragement, information, and updated material on conflict and conflict management, please check out our web site at **www.conflictdynamics.org**

Notes

Managing Conflict Dynamics:

A Practical Approach

Building Relationships

- Treat everyone as a client — with respect, courtesy, concern and appreciation.

- Foster an atmosphere of open communication and accessibility.

- Listen more than you talk.

- Show you CARE: Compliment, Appreciate, Reward, Encourage.

- Value differences and diversity.

Managing Emotions

- Provide Triple A emotional services: Anticipate, Acknowledge, Apologize.

- Control your emotions; don't let them control you.

- Chill out with time out.

- Channel your emotional energy in constructive directions.

- Choose to feel differently.

Resolving Conflict

- Attack problems, not people.

- Build consensus, not conflict.

- Communicate.

- Cooperate.

- Collaborate.

Accepting Conflict

- Be self-confident, not self-critical.

- Act professionally and ethically.

- Adjust, adapt, improve.

- Accentuate the positive.

- Acknowledge that some conflicts can't be resolved.

Mottos

- When I listen, people talk.
- Constructive criticism curbs conflict.
- Choose to chill.
- Break down barriers; build bridges.
- Feel the fear and do it anyway.
- Q-TIP — Quit Taking It Personally!
- Confront conflict constructively.

- TLC — Think, Listen, Communicate.
- Time out, not cop out.
- If I lose it, I lose.
- Express it, don't suppress it.
- Win one for everyone.
- Nothing can bring you peace but yourself.
- Know when to say when.

Words To Live By

When anger rises, think of the consequences.   (*Confucius*)

Hear the other side.   (*St. Augustine*)

If indeed you must be candid, be candid beautifully.   (*K. Gibran*)

Be civil to all; sociable to many; familiar with few; friend to one; enemy to none.   (*B. Franklin*)

Notes

 Resources

Conflict Websites

humanresources.about.com
About.com: Human Resources features articles and links on developing effective work relationships and overcoming workplace negativity.

www.confidencecenter.com
Confidence Center provides articles, seminars, coaching and resources on improving employee morale and performance.

www.workteams.unt.edu
Center for Collaborative Organizations features articles, a newsletter and a listserv discussion group on team-related topics.

www.angermgmt.com/
angermgmt.com provides a toolkit for measuring anger along with advice, resources, trainings and a blog.

www.chacocanyon.com
Chaco Canyon Consulting features essays, an e-mail newsletter and workshops on many topics related to workplace relationships, stresses and conflict.

www.resource-i.com/Articles/UnderstandingEmotion.htm
Article "Understanding Emotions in the Workplace" defines key emotions and outlines a nine-step process for mastering them.

www.work911.com
Work911 Workplace Supersite presents articles, resources and training on many workplace issues including preventing and managing conflict.

www.projectmechanics.com/conflict-resolution.html
Project Mechanics features articles, links, resources and a blog on conflict resolution and project management.

www.mediationworks.com/pubs/index.html
Mediation Training Institute International provides a technique for measuring the financial costs of conflict, articles on conflict management, seminar materials and training opportunities.

www.robertpennington.com/handout.html
Resource International provides information on managing workplace stress and anxiety as well as audio, video and web-based trainings and executive coaching.

www.zeromillion.com/personaldev/
ZeroMillion.com features articles and resources on adapting to or overcoming workplace challenges.

www.realscienceofsuccess.com
Positive Psychology provides science-based tools and strategies for self-improvement, personal growth and success.

www.relationships911.org
Relationships911.org features a newsletter, articles and resources on understanding personality and learning styles and defusing difficult people.

www.diffcon.com/wordpress/index.php
Triad Consulting Group presents links to articles and a blog as companions to its book, *Difficult Conversations: How to Discuss What Matters Most.*

www.bullyonline.org
Bully OnLine provides links, resources and information on workplace bullying, its effects and how to address it.

See also *Resources* at www.conflictdynamics.org

Conflict Seminars

Leadership Development Institute, Eckerd College, phone: 800-753-0444, www.eckerd.edu/ldi
- Emphasis: Development of conflict management skills through assessment, interactive learning and action-oriented individual development plans.
- Services: Programs and workshops in St. Petersburg, Florida, in-house custom programs, executive coaching.
- Seminars: *Resolving Conflict Effectively; Leadership, Conflict & Negotiation; Learning Through Mediation.*

Center for Creative Leadership, phone: 336-545-2810, www.ccl.org/programs
- Emphasis: Advancing the understanding, practice and development of leadership.
- Services: Open-enrollment and customized programs offered around the world.
- Seminars: *Foundations of Leadership; The Looking Glass Experience; Navigating Complex Challenges; Leadership & High-Performance Teams.*

Mediation Training Institute International, phone: 888-222-3271, www.mediationworks.com
- Emphasis: Prevention and early resolution of workplace conflict through core competencies.
- Services: On-line and in-house training; seminars offered around the world.
- Seminars: *How to Mediate Employee Conflict: The Manager-as-Mediator; How to Resolve Conflict with Others: The Self-as-Mediator.*

Program on Negotiation, Executive Education Series, Harvard Law School, phone: 781-239-1111, www.pon.execseminars.com
- Emphasis: Theory and practice of negotiation and dispute resolution.
- Services: Seminars and programs conducted at Harvard.
- Seminars: *How to Say No & Still Get to Yes; Managing the Difficult Business Conversation; Dealing with Difficult People & Difficult Situations; Dealing with Emotions in Business Negotiations; Program on Negotiation for Senior Executives.*

VitalSmarts, phone: 800-449-5989, vitalsmarts.com.
- Emphasis: Building teams and interpersonal skills to improve performance.
- Services: Web seminars, trainings, keynote speaking, on-site consulting, executive team development.
- Seminars: *Crucial Confrontations™; Crucial Conversations®.*

Triad Consulting Group, phone: 617-547-1728, www.triadcgi.com
- Emphasis: Improving performance, collaboration and problem-solving through better communication.
- Services: Customized corporate education, open workshops, executive coaching, facilitated conversations.
- Seminars: *Managing Difficult Business Conversations; Negotiating for Results; Advanced Negotiation: Difficult Tactics; Delivering Bad News.*

Center for Collaborative Organizations, phone: 940-565-3096, www.workteams.unt.edu
- Emphasis: Building collaborative work systems and enhancing teaming.
- Services: Conferences, public workshops, customized on-site training.
- Seminars: *Collaborative Problem Solving; Best Team Skills; Facilitation is Leadership in Action.*

CareerTrack/Fred Pryor Seminars, phone: 800-780-8476, www.pryor.com.
- Emphasis: Convenient and practical business-skills training.
- Services: On-line and on-site seminars; public workshops around the U.S.
- Seminars: *Effective Communication Skills for Managing Conflict & Confrontation; Criticis & Discipline Skills for Managers & Supervisors; Managing Emotions Under Pressure; Deali with Difficult People; How to Deal with Unacceptable Employee Behavior.*

See also Resources at www.conflictdynamics.org

Conflict Books

The Art of Managing: How to Build a Better Workplace and Relationships,
T. M. Jane, 2007, Infinity. A guide to more effective management and communication styles.

Teaching an Anthill to Fetch: Developing Collaborative Intelligence @ Work,
S. J. Joyce, 2007, Mighty Small Books. How to build teams and create collaborative, purposeful situations.

Discussing the Undiscussable: A Guide to Overcoming Defensive Routines in the Workplace, W. Noonan, 2007, Jossey-Bass. Exercises for detecting and discussing defensive routines in a safe, productive way.

Toxic Emotions at Work and What You Can Do About Them, P. J. Frost, 2007, Harvard Business School. How individuals and organizations have successfully managed negative emotions.

Emotions at Work: Theory, Research and Applications for Management,
R. L. Payne & C. Cooper, 2007, Wiley-Interscience. How negative and positive emotions impinge upon organizations and their workforces.

The Power of a Positive No: How to Say No and Still Get to Yes, W. Ury, 2007, Bantam. Managing accommodation, attacking and avoiding through the "Positive No." This book is a companion to two classics, ***Getting to Yes: Negotiating Agreement without Giving In***, 1981, and ***Getting Ready to Negotiate***, 1995.

Conflict Resolution for Managers and Leaders (Participants Workbook from CDR Associates Training Package), CDR Associates, 2007, Jossey-Bass. A program on the keys to conflict management, negotiation and dispute resolution.

Renaissance 5002 Guide: Making the Most of Conflict, D. Mashia et al. (Eds.), 2007, Renaissance Professional Training. Understanding why conflicts happen, how to mitigate their severity and deal with difficult people.

Your Survival Strategies Are Killing You: The Eight Principles You Must Follow to Thrive in Life and Work, M. Borst, 2007, Avista. Assessment tools and principles for effective communication, teamwork, productivity and balance.

Run With the Bulls Without Getting Trampled: The Qualities You Need to Stay Out of Harm's Way and Thrive at Work, T. Irwin, 2007, Thomas Nelson. Traits and strategies for success and personal fulfillment.

Five Good Minutes at Work: 100 Mindful Practices to Help You Relieve Stress & Bring Your Best to Work, B. Jeffery & W. Millstine, 2007, New Harbinger. Exercises and visualizations to stay calm, focused and re-vitalized at work.

Toxic People: Decontaminate Difficult People at Work without Using Weapons or Duct Tape, M. Petrie Sue, 2007, Wiley. Solutions for dealing with difficult people and the conflict and miscommunication they create.

From Difficult to Disturbed: Understanding and Managing Dysfunctional Employees, L. Miller, 2007, AMACOM/American Management Association. Solutions for dealing with difficult personalities and employees with mental disorders.

Becoming a Conflict Competent Leader: How You and Your Organization Can Manage Conflict Effectively, C. E. Runde & T. A. Flanagan, 2006, Jossey-Bass (Center for Creative Leadership). A guide to the skills Conflict Competent Leaders need to help themselves, their colleagues and their organizations deal more effectively with conflict.

How to Win Friends and Influence People, D. Carnegie, 1981 (revised edition), Pocket Books. First published in 1936, this classic is still relevant today.

See also *Resources* at **www.conflictdynamics.org**
